Real Gone Girls

Darla Pugh

Published by Trellis Publishing, 2021.

While every precaution has been taken in the preparation of this book, the publisher assumes no responsibility for errors or omissions, or for damages resulting from the use of the information contained herein.

REAL GONE GIRLS

First edition. July 15, 2021.

Copyright © 2021 Darla Pugh.

ISBN: 979-8224974917

Written by Darla Pugh.

REAL GONE GIRLS

DIANE PUGH

MICHELLE THEER

At first glance, Michelle Theer looked like the stereotypical bored housewife. She married an Air Force captain who was deployed on assignment for long periods of time. Her days were spent alone and idle.

And you know what they say about idle hands.

Michelle felt unfulfilled in her marriage and didn't so much want out, she wanted something more. Attractive with long brown hair and arched eyebrows, Michelle did not have any problems attracting members of the opposite sex. She needed something discreet, however, something that would simply titillate her fantasies and relief the boredom that she would suffer during the long absences of her husband.

So she turned to the Internet.

It started innocently at first. A few keystrokes of flirtatious messages. Some a bit racier than others, but where was the harm? She was hiding behind a computer monitor. It isn't cheating if there is no face to face, Michelle thought.

Then she came across the profile of John Diamond. His pictures showed him to be a tall and muscular man, a special forces soldier that made Michelle's heart skip a beat.

Or maybe she saw him as the perfect foil. The perfect fall guy to get rid of her husband.

Their flirtations started innocently enough. Then the messages got racier and racier until they both felt the need to satiate their fantasies for one another.

Those fantasies led to sex.

Then murder.

Frank Theer, better known as "Marty", was a quiet and reserved young man. In high school, his friends introduced him to what they believed what be his perfect match.

Michelle Forcier.

Michelle was outgoing, bubbly and only sixteen when she met Marty who was a year older. Her friends believed that Michelle's extroverted personality could be a counterweight to Marty's introverted nature. Marty had originally intended to become an astronaut, his ambition and intelligence made him an attractive catch to Michelle. They were both the product of military families, both moving a lot as children so they had a kinship there. Both were ambitious and had concrete plans for the future. Marty would join the Air Force. Michelle would join the reserves and serve in the Gulf War.

"Michelle had ambition," forensic psychologist Paula Orange said. "She wanted status and respect. But she grew up in a military family and succumbed to the tribalism and social pressures that existed in that kind of environment. You grow up, get married and have kids. Michelle probably had mixed feelings about that. She wanted to do her own thing. So, in essence, she was living a double life from the get-go. She was doing the expected thing of getting married but on the side she was the libertine, drinking heavily and having extra-marital affairs."

The couple would maintain their long-distance relationship for four years until Michelle was assigned to the Persian Gulf War in 1991. Thinking that their courtship had lasted long enough, Marty asked Michelle to marry him.

Michelle, at twenty years old, said yes to the other man she had known up until that point.

Their wedding video would show the couple to be a happy one. They kissed for the cameras and fed each other wedding cake.

"We did everything together," Michelle said. "He treated me really well. I just thought we had the perfect relationship. We were best friends."

The couple would remain married for six years as Marty's Air Force assignments forced them to move from base to base. Michelle had fantasized about going to exotic locations overseas. Instead, Marty's tenure was limited to uninspiring outposts in Oklahoma, Alabama and Florida.

Places that would bore Michelle to tears.

"Michelle was getting lonely," Orange said. "Like so many military families, these things take shape early on. Marty would be gone months at a time and of course telephone and e-mail exchanges are not the same as a face to face. Michelle felt entitled to more from life then what she was getting. This isn't uncommon obviously but Michelle took things one step further eventually."

During the occasions when Marty was on leave, he and Michelle would often end up fighting.

"I want children," Marty said.

"No way," Michelle would shake her head, stifling a laugh.

"Then what's the point? What's the point of being married if we are not going to start a family?"

"Raise children in this shithole? You've got to be kidding."

The arguments would escalate. Michelle was a slob, refusing to clean up around the house. Marty would complain but Michelle would deflect and criticize him for his poor career choice.

"You're never home," Michelle hissed. "And you want a family?"

After nine years of marriage, Marty was sent to the Pope Air Force Base near Fayetteville, North Carolina. Fayetteville was considered to be the equivalent of Siberia when it came to transfers. Military members gave the town nicknames like FayetteNam, Fatalville, and FayetteHell. Michelle found the town to be even worse than its reputation when it came to providing excitement.

"Here I was in Fayetteville," Michelle said. "'Loserville'. And I had nobody I could hang out with. Nobody I could pick up a phone and call."

Marty saw things differently, writing on a Christmas card in 2000, "Pope has provided a great change of pace for me and Michelle is happy with her new job. So, 2000 is looking good for both of us."

Michelle would suffer from depression and loneliness after the six years of marriage. Marty tried hard to appease his high-maintenance wife. He took her scuba diving in the Caribbean, skiing in the Rockies, parachuting in Georgia and then a summer marathon run in Alaska.

Despite all of the adventures, Michelle was dissatisfied. She wanted something more out of life, more excitement. She decided to go back to school and earn a degree in psychology. She felt desperately alone, however, as Marty would once again be deployed overseas. Michelle would find work with a psychologist named Dr. Thomas Harbin's and work to obtain her license in psychology.

Still, it wasn't enough. She needed excitement.

More specifically, sexual excitement.

So she turned to the Internet.

Michelle began turning to dating sites. She noodled around with different memberships and it never became more than an idle pursuit to fill the hours of loneliness. Setting up her ad with the headline of "sexy brunette seeks rendezvous man", her inbox was immediately deluged with drooling suitors.

She entertained a number of different men, sending and receiving flirty messages. Michelle had become interested in the local "swinger" and sex club scene, advertising for a man who would be her escort to a club called "Carolina Friends."

One man got her attention more than the others.

JOHN DIAMOND

John was four years younger than Michelle, entering the United States Army during the year in which the couple got married. He had a wandering eye, currently married to his second wife knew of his lothario ways. She was a Panamanian woman who was a few years older than John. He didn't hide his infidelities and on one occasion had one of his girlfriends call the house to ask his wife if John was still meeting her at the beach.

"John loved women," Debbie Dvorak, John's younger sister said. "He loved women, he always had a girlfriend and was a ladies man. My brother was an attractive guy. He had a great personality. His personality made him that much more attractive."

John's background was remarkably similar to Marty in that he was born into a military family. His father was a Vietnam veteran and his grandfather had been a POW during World War II. John himself became an Army ranger and was stationed nearby at Fort Bragg. He was trained as a sniper and highly decorated. Their military backgrounds were where their similarities ended, however. Marty was highly respected as a pilot and a family man. John was a good soldier but nowhere near the honorable family man Marty was.

"John was a highly regarded soldier," Orange said. "But he already had two families. He had a child with his first wife and they divorced. He remarried and had a son with the second wife. So his plate was already full by the time he met Michelle Theer."

John and Michelle both intuitively knew what the other wanted. They both needed the adrenaline, the excitement of forbidden sex to add spice to their humdrum lives. John and Michelle spent months sending each other flirtatious and juicy e-mails before realizing it was time to put fantasy aside and meet for real.

There was an immediate attraction as they met at a Fayetteville coffee shop.

"It was love at first sight," John said.

"I thought he was very, very charming," Michelle said. "He was funny. We talked about movies and music. Things that me and Marty didn't talk about."

They were both still married, however, and that added to the thrill.

LET THE SEDUCTION BEGIN

John and Michelle then began spending as much time with they could with one another. Their extra-marital affair could be done inside Michelle's own bedroom as Marty would be stationed overseas. Michelle grew addicted to the sex, the excitement and the adoration that John gave her.

"He was very attentive," Michelle said. "He was very affectionate. He was very adoring. Yeah, it felt great."

The sex grew addicting for both John and Michelle. Like drug addicts, they found escape through the pleasures of the flesh. E-mails and text messages between the two would reveal a controlling relationship that favored Michelle. He was at her beck and call, like a "puppy dog" said one investigator.

"I can't wait until you come back so we can take care of each other," John wrote in one message. "You know, sex, sex, sex and of course...more sex. I know that we are meant to be together and are kindred soul mates. I will always love you, no matter how you have hurt me."

"I think it was just the sex," Dvorak said when asked what John saw in the married Michelle. "He was obsessed. He was smitten with having sex with her."

Michelle would later reveal to her psychologist that she didn't think that the affair took away from her love for Marty.

"She said that Marty was the love of her life," Orange said. "With John, it was just lust. She never loved him the same way she loved Marty. At least that is how she differentiated and rationalized it in her mind."

Without fear of being caught, the two began going to dance clubs as well as "swinger parties" as a couple at Michelle's request.

"She would take him to these sex clubs," Dvorak said. "She would say 'If you want to go have sex with her, that's okay. That's fine. Go. I'm fine with it.' And he was just like 'Wow, okay.'"

Finding a partner in crime for her sex addiction, Michelle indulged whenever she could.

Then Marty returned home.

REPAIR JOB?

Marty had been undergoing flight maneuvers in Little Rock, Arkansas. When he returned home to Fayetteville, he came back knowing that his marriage was on the rocks. Michelle wanted to go to marriage counseling but Marty refused.

"He wouldn't agree to marriage counseling and I moved out," Michelle said. "He was shocked."

Michelle got her own place that summer. She would spend most of her days and nights in the arms of John Diamond. "He was so attentive," Michelle recalled. "He would rub my feet for five hours if I wanted him to."

John continued to fall deeper in love with Michelle. He thought that she was more intelligent than the women he had dated before, more of a challenge. Three months after living alone, however, Michelle changed her mind about John.

She went back to Marty.

Michelle thought she would give the marriage one more chance. Marty relented on going to counseling and the couple hashed things out with the therapist.

"I want Michelle to clean up around the house more," Marty said to the counselor. "I mean, I know that with women's lib and all that sounds very degrading. But I work my tail off. I'm away for months at a time and would at least like to come home to someplace clean. It shows respect. Coming home to a mess of a house shows a lot of disrespect."

"See what I mean?" Michelle said. "Talk about obsessive-compulsive. Where does a clean house fit in the grand scheme of things? I want to live life. Go out and have new experiences.

But this guy? All he wants to do is stay home. Stay home in his clean house."

The counseling didn't work. In the summer of 2000, Michelle moved out of the family home. She and John found an off-base apartment and began living together. The cheating couple took a vacation to the Netherlands Antilles and fell in love with the place. Michelle enjoyed it so much that she applied to the Saba School of Medicine. She listed John as her next of kin, describing his relationship to her as "fiancee".

But later Michelle would tell her psychologist that her decision to go back with John was a "relapse."

"I knew that I loved Marty," Michelle said. "And I knew that I wanted to make it work. I knew it in my heart."

Then she went back to Marty again.

She continued to see John, however, but the relationship would be on and off. John would plead his case through e-mails, writing flowery messages about how much he loved Michelle.

"I love you so much," John wrote. "I know you feel the same. What I don't understand is how you could be with a man that you don't love anymore. You're unhappy with him. You're happy with me. This is all so confusing."

"He said specifically 'I'm going to kill myself,' Michelle said. "'I can't live without you. You can't do this to me. I'm gonna go drive my car off a bridge.'"

According to Michelle, John would not relent in his pursuit of her. He would show up at her office and make a scene, telling her that he would tell Marty about their affair.

Michelle relented to seeing John one last time, agreeing to meet with John at a local restaurant. According to her statements to her psychologist, she went there in the hopes of ending the affair for good.

"We had that whole talk," Michelle said. "You know, 'we can only be friends' and 'this can never happen again. Never, never, never.' He seemed very calm. Very rational. I told him, 'I don't want to leave my husband.' I never told him, 'I love you.' I never said 'I want to be with you.' I mean, I think I was pretty straight up."

Whether this conversation took place or not, it certainly landed on deaf ears to John. He continued to pursue Michelle and they continued to see one another.

"She probably led him on a roller coaster ride of emotions," military investigator Vincent Bustillo said. "Brought him to the peak, thinking everything was going to be good and they're going to leave this life together, off in some Caribbean island, and then back off and leave Diamond emotionally distraught to the point where that's what he wanted and nothing was going to get in his way."

The on-again, off-again relationship turned red hot by December 9th, 2000. Michelle told Marty that she would be attending a birthday party for a graduate school friend of hers. Thinking nothing of it, Marty simply nodded his head.

Michelle left the home and met John for a night of torrid sex.

"The manipulation began early on in the relationship," Orange said. "Michelle would pull John into her world with sex. Then she would push him away by going back to her husband. John was smitten with her and could not let go. He would have done anything for her and Michelle knew it. An Army ranger willing to do anything for you is a powerful thing. It was like having her own personal soldier willing to kill. But who did she need getting rid of and why?"

Michelle knew that Marty had a half-million dollar insurance policy that he took out in 1999.

She was the sole beneficiary.

John's sister, however, remained adamant that Michelle had written those lovelorn letters to herself in order to put the trail on John Diamond.

"He never once expressed any feelings of love for her to me," Debbie Dvorak said. "Unless you come to me with a handwritten letter that he was obsessed with her, I'll never believe that. He told me he did not want to marry her. He did not want to spend the rest of his life with her. I think she was obsessed with him. Obsessed that she couldn't control him. That she couldn't control the situation."

Eight days later after her latest rendezvous, Michelle would attend a Christmas party given by her employer, Dr. Thomas Harbin. She brought along Marty who seemed to enjoy the company at the otherwise mellow party. About an hour into the get-together, Michelle excused herself to make a phone call.

A phone call to John Diamond.

A short while later, Marty and Michelle drove another couple home before heading to the local gas station.

"We ended up turning around and going back to the office," Michelle said. "To get some stuff that I needed so I could stay up and work that night."

Marty sat in their Ford Explorer and watched as Michelle walked up to the second story office. A few minutes passed and Marty got worried. He got out of the car and went upstairs to her office to make sure his wife was okay.

He reached the top of the stairs and then he was ambushed.

A gunman stepped out from the shadows and fired four times. Marty tumbled down the stairwell. When he reached the bottom, he was still alive.

The shadowy gunman stood above him and fired one more time, killing Marty.

Michelle would state to police that she discovered Marty's body and began screaming his name. She said that she thought he was still breathing but in the haste of living her office she locked her keys inside. Michelle said she ran two miles to a video store to call 911 despite the area having numerous homes and businesses nearby.

Police arrived on scene and found Michelle cradling Marty in her arms, her husband's blood pooling onto the concrete. Military police arrived shortly after the city authorities, getting the case after it was revealed that Marty was an Air Force Captain.

Both police agencies initially suspected that Marty was the victim of a random robbery. They searched the area and found no one despite the fact that Michelle stated that she has "seen someone in the bushes" when she discovered Marty's body.

FIGURING THINGS OUT

Investigators would discover bullet holes at the top of the stairwell as well as sequins from Marty's suit. They surmised that Marty was at the top of the stairwell when he was shot from someone coming from the bottom of the steps. He then fell down the stairs, bleeding but still alive when the attacker delivered the fatal shot to the back of his left ear.

The police then found his wallet with cash and credit cards still on his person. The scene now looked less like a robbery and more like a targeted execution. After recovering the shell casings (a 9mm pistol was the culprit) they went upstairs to Michelle's office. Inside, they discovered that Michelle had used the toilet (and didn't flush) as well as leaving an empty candy wrapper in the trash.

Police noted that it was almost as if she went upstairs to wait *something* out. If she were, in fact, looking for a book, it would not have taken that long.

The police released Michelle on her own recognizance. The next morning, they returned to the office and spoke to her employer, Dr. Harbin. The doctor would reveal that Michelle had been having marital trouble and was having an affair with John Diamond.

Police now saw John Diamond as the man with the motive. But when they interviewed Lourdes Diamond, John's wife, she said that she was home with her husband that entire evening, watching a movie. The police became discouraged.

Then Lourdes added that John got a call about 9 p.m. that evening and that he quickly left the house. She stated that John changed his clothes, put on parka clothing and told her that he had to go to the barracks.

Police then checked out the phone records on John's cell phone and noted that he did receive a call from Michelle.

Michelle would later deny that she ever called John that night.

After receiving the cell phone records, however, it became evident that John and Michelle had called each other twenty times a day at a minimum. They had exchanged a phone call about ninety minutes prior to Marty being shot to death.

When pressed on his involvement with Michelle, John admitted to the affair.

"She is one of many," John said. "She's a side piece. I have a lot of women."

Michelle would later claim that she conducted her own detective work after Marty's death. She stated that she went to John's home and asked him if he knew anything about the murder.

"I asked him 'do you know anything about this," Michelle said. "'Do you know anybody who had anything to do with this?' He said 'No, I would never do anything to hurt you. I know how much you loved him.' I believed him. He looked so trustful."

Police would dismiss Michelle's confrontation with John. They tailed him around town, watching him park in front of the Theer home and sneak inside through the back door.

John would remain there the whole night.

"He knew I was depressed," Michelle said. "And I was getting more and more depressed. I think I went to John for comfort."

John and Michelle would then travel to Florida as Marty's murder investigation was ongoing. The official reason according to Michelle:

Grief counseling.

She claimed there was a former professor there in the state that would be able to help her cope with Marty's death.

While in Florida, John went to live with his sister, Debbie Dvorak.

"He acted as if nothing was wrong," Dvorak said. "He knows he had nothing to do with it. He didn't shoot him."

The physical evidence remained weak. The police continued to sift through the cell phone records and came across the phone number of one of John's army friends. Calling him up, they asked if John would have access to any 9mm weaponry. The friend would reveal that he had, in fact, loaned out his gun to John. The transaction took place just days before Marty's murder. The Smith & Wesson Model 5906 that he loaned John would be the same type of weapon used to kill Marty. All the police had to do was obtain the murder weapon and they would have the physical evidence required to indict.

Then, as if on cue in a mystery movie, John Diamond reported a break-in of his car in the base parking lot.

"Did they steal anything?" a reporting officer asked.

"Yeah," John said. "My friend's gun. Jesus, he's going to be pissed."

But John made a mistake.

There was a pile of glass outside the car which would indicate that the passenger side door had been open during the "break-in". John had smashed the window himself and feared getting glass on the interior of his car.

The US Army investigators would charge John with obstruction of justice, conspiracy, and premeditated murder. The Army officials relayed their findings to civilian police and wanted them to charge Michelle. Five months later, John would be court-martialed. Michelle would be called as a witness but invoke her Fifth Amendment right with every question.

"John would have a cocky air about him throughout his trial," Orange said. "He joked with reporters and smiled at the jury. He felt certain that he would be acquitted."

His cocky demeanor would backfire. The jury would find John guilty and he was convicted of all counts. His current wife Lourdes would testify that John would receive a phone call in the evening and leave the home. His mother-in-law would also testify that he had come home in the middle of the night and began washing clothes.

John would be sentenced to life without parole.

But Michelle Theer remained free.

"What I got from him (John) after he was arrested was that he didn't want anything to do with her," his sister Debbie said. "Nothing. You don't expect to be convicted on theory. On myths. Show me blood. Show me a gun. Show me a time-line that works. Show me those facts. I'll believe until the day I die that she (Michelle) killed her husband, that she planned to have my brother go down for it, so she could live this happy, wonderful life."

"From my opinion, if he (John) wanted to shoot someone he could have shot someone from a mile away. Why sneak up on somebody and shoot them five times and even according to the coroner, they're all over the place. Whoever shot that weapon wasn't a sharp shooter. Didn't know how to shoot a weapon, was scared to be there, whatever, they were all over the place. Ricocheting off of this and ricocheting off of that. There's just no way."

Upon John's conviction, Michelle left town. She moved to New Orleans until the Fayetteville police finally got the grand jury to indict her on charges of first-degree murder in May of 2002.

Michelle fled the city, however, and became a fugitive on the run.

"I think she planned to kill her husband a long time ago," Dvorak said. "I think she waited and researched and waited for that right person who would look and fit the part to pin it on."

During John's trial, Michelle had begun her preparation. She purchased pamphlets such as REBORN IN THE USA, HOW TO DISAPPEAR IN AMERICA, and SECRETS FOR GETTING A NEW IDENTITY, obtaining tips on how to evade detection from authorities. Michelle also obtained a few books on learning Spanish and travel guides to several Latin countries like Mexico. She bleached her hair blonde and used a high-end printer to make both fake birth and baptismal certificates.

Michelle was dead serious about evading capture. Hiding out in Florida, she paid to have plastic surgery done on her nose, chin and had laser surgery to remove her acne and other skin blemishes.

From an appearance standpoint, she had fully reinvented herself. Michelle was able to fool the DMV and get a driver's license under the alias of "Alexandra Solomon." She rented an apartment under the name of "Lisa Pendragon" from Cynthia Geesey in Lauderdale by the Sea, Florida.

"She told me that she was on the run from an abusive boyfriend in California," Geesey said. "I thought she was well-spoken and articulate."

Geesey allowed Michelle to sign the six-month lease, believing her story. Michelle would blend into her surroundings rather easily. She made a few friends around the neighborhood and found a new boyfriend. She then called her parents from a pay phone in town to let them know she was okay.

"She was always a little apprehensive," Geesey said. "Always looking over her shoulder. That's the only thing I found a little strange about her. I was talking to her one day in front of her apartment and there was a helicopter overhead. And she freaked out! Ran back inside. I said 'It's just a helicopter' and she said 'I don't know, it might be my boyfriend.' And I found that a little odd. But other than that she seemed pretty reasonable , paid her rent on time. Took good care of her animals, no other problems with her."

Fayetteville police were at a loss in locating Michelle and enlisted the aid of United States Marshals. True to form, they knew that Michelle could not resist male companionship and caught a break. Michelle instructed her new boyfriend to call her parents from a pay phone in order to relay a message. Her new beau, however, made the mistake of calling Michelle's family from his parent's home. The U.S. Marshals were already tracing all of Michelle's calls and they quickly found out the identity of her new boyfriend.

Placing him under watch, Michelle's new beau soon led authorities straight to her.

After being on the run for three months, Michelle had been finally been captured.

THE AFTERMATH

Michelle's case took two years to go to trial. She would turn down a plea deal which would send her to prison for only ten years. The case then went to trial for ten weeks, drawing both local and national media attention.

Despite the lengthy trial, the jury returned after only six hours of deliberation.

Marty Theer's mother, Linda, waited in nervous anticipation as the verdict was read.

"Guilty."

Linda shook with emotion and tears as the word was spoken. For her, she felt relief that the trial was finally over.

"He (Marty) was a very, very tender person," Linda said. "There wasn't a mean bone in his body. He wouldn't have anything bad to say about anybody. I wish I could say the same."

Michelle would be sentenced to life in prison without the possibility of parole. She is currently housed at the North Carolina Correctional Institute for Women in Raleigh, North Carolina.

John is currently imprisoned at the United States Disciplinary Barracks at Fort Leavenworth, Kansas.

Both John and Michelle have made attempts to obtain a new trial without success.

LINDA MCELROY

19

BELLA WILLIAMS

At first glance, Linda McElroy looked to be another ordinary house cleaner.

Sixty-four years old, overweight and with glasses, she had settled into an anonymous life in Pulaski, Tennessee.

"She blended into the community," forensic psychologist Paula Orange said. "Her employers all said the same thing about her. That she was a delight. Hard-working, friendly, and trustworthy."

McElroy had remained in small, rural town of Pulaski for over thirty-five years. The reputation she had earned was hard-won.

No one knew about her previous life.

She was a convicted murderer.

But now she was for all intents and purposes, a respected member of the community. A wife, mother and now grandmother to eight grandchildren.

Unassuming and harmless.

But the thirty-five years had to have been tortuous ones for McElroy. Any unexpected knock on the door must have sent her heart racing. Any police siren in the distance must have sent her on edge.

Could this be the day?

The day when the authorities finally catch up with her.

In 2007, they finally did.

THE CRIME

Linda made her home in the riverside city of Ashland, Kentucky in 1961. She was eighteen years old and had four children early in her teen years. She and her growing brood were doomed to a life of poverty in the small Kentucky town.

"Linda wasn't particularly attractive," Orange said. "She wasn't ugly but she certainly could attract men when she wanted. Little is known about her early life as far as what type of childhood she had and what type of student she was. From what we can gather, however, she was damn good at attracting enablers. People who would look the other way when she would misbehave. Even her own parents harbored her at one point she from an early age you can surmise that she didn't encounter much in the way of discipline."

Linda, like most women her age in rural Kentucky, wanted more out of life. But in the town of Ashland, there were not a whole lot of opportunities. So she did what most women her age did.

She got pregnant.

"She was known as a 'good time girl,'" Orange said. "Or what in today's parlance would be called a 'party girl.' Linda wanted it both ways. She wanted a family and she also wanted to do her own thing and hang out with her girlfriends. Which, of course, led to meeting different men as well."

Linda left her then husband one night, telling him that she was off to meet her girlfriends. The two would argue. He wanted her home. She wanted out after spending all day with the children.

"Where do you think you're going?"

"Out," she replied.

"Out? You've got four children. Count them, one, two three-"

"And I stay home all damn day and take care of them," Linda said. "You go out-"

"I work-"

"And I don't?"

"You stay your ass home," her husband said.

"No, you stay your ass home," Linda said, looking at the man with disgust. "You're going nowhere and taking me with you. No thank you, that is what I say. No, thank you."

Linda would lock herself in the bathroom. Then she would come out, thirty minutes later all dolled up for a night on the town.

"The two would engage in horrific fights," Orange said. "They were more psychological than physical. He wanted a stay at home wife. She wanted none of that. She had a rapidly fading youth and she was seeing her entire life slip away. So they would argue. Stay home or go out and party."

Linda would always win the arguments.

She would find a new boyfriend in seventeen-year-old Charles Darby. He fell for Linda hook, line and sinker despite the fact she had four children.

Charles had a reputation in town as a serious young man, a good student who was a hard worker. He was in the Navy for a brief spell and served aboard the USS Enterprise. He had seen parts of the world that Linda had only dreamed about, a far cry from the ball and chain that awaited her at the house.

Linda would play on the young man's sympathies, telling him of her rotten home life.

"Do you really love him?" Charles asked.

"I thought I did," Linda said. "No, I don't know. I mean, I want what is best for the kids."

"There's no way we can keep going on like this."

"I know. I hate going back there. I hate leaving you for him."

"So do the opposite."

"What do you mean?"

"Leave him for me."

"For good?"

"Yes."

The two kissed and sealed their deal. Linda would divorce her husband for Charles and they would settle into a life where they would live happily ever after.

"Linda would play upon the chivalry of the young Charles," Orange said. "She established herself as the sympathetic figure, the damsel in distress. Charles was a nice guy. He saw himself as better than the man that Linda was currently with. So he 'stepped up', so to speak. Little did he know that a fate that awaited him was much worse."

Word of their affair spread and the cheating couple was shunned by the neighbors and friends.

In 1962, Linda would divorce her husband and marry Charles. The newlywed couple would move all the way to Hammond, Indiana in order to get far removed from both of their families in Kentucky.

The union would last over seven years before Charles began being bogged down by bills. Linda had brought her four children from her previous marriage into the relationship and the couple had an additional child of their own, Charles Jr, aka "Chuckie."

Neither parent was a big earner. Linda did not have a regular job while Charles worked as a "freelance carpenter" as well as putting in the aluminum siding on houses. Both were described as hard-working by neighbors, with Linda being described as a "meticulous housewife" and a "good mother."

"Linda was a classic entitlement case," Orange said. "She would take what little money the couple had and would treat herself. Clothes, shoes, furniture. She would treat herself before paying any bills. Then that is when the trouble started. The gas went out. The lights went out."

Charles went ballistic when he discovered Linda wasn't paying the bills.

She then revealed to Charles that she had "cancer" and had used the money to pay for her doctor bills.

The ruse worked.

Charles, a sensitive type, immediately broke down in tears and guilt. He didn't have insurance as a self-employed carpenter and felt he wasn't fulfilling his obligation as a provider.

"Linda was the type to make up whatever story she needed," Orange said. "She wanted money. When she told Charles that she had cancer she did it in order to extract more money out of him."

Charles soon found out that Linda's cancer story was a lie.

"He kept pestering her about her cancer," Orange said. "Eventually, the ruse cracked. It had to. Charles was a dutiful man who would have wanted to do right by a sickly wife. He would have been the type to take her to weekly chemotherapy treatments and be the doting husband. But when she revealed that it was all a lie. A lie to cover-up her bad money habits that must have devastated him. He felt as if he had been played and he saw no way out. Linda, on the other hand, was all about finding an escape route. She had no conscience and didn't care about anything."

He then took out an ad in the newspaper, revealing to the public that he was not responsible for Linda's debt.

The advertisement read:

"I, Charles Darby disavow any future debts incurred by my wife, Linda Darby, who is guilty of lying and overspending."

The public humiliation did little to heal things between the young couple. The two quickly became enemies and Linda privately vowed revenge.

"Charles was a nice guy," Orange said. "He got caught up into caring for a woman who really cared only for herself. So he got trapped in a really bad situation. He could have left her with the four children but had the one biological child with Linda. So he felt a sense of duty that would ultimately prove to be fatal."

"Taking out an ad in the paper was a smart move by Charles in hindsight," Orange said. "He set the stage for the public to see the kind of person Linda was. There were on a limited budget and rather than using the money for the children she would use the money on herself. So he was able to establish the fact that he was the responsible one. She could not use the 'battered wife' defense against Charles because he was for all intents and purposes, a good guy that was covering his tracks."

The couple had been subjected to vandalism and threats but police chalked those incidents up to Linda. Someone had spray painted graffiti on their homes and threatened the household with phone calls.

Police determined that the perpetrator was Linda in both of those cases in bizarre attempts to scare Charles and the children.

A TIME FOR POISON

Charles would then come down with a mysterious illness following his public disclaimer in the newspaper. He remained bed-ridden for some time, unable to rid himself of the illness.

Linda doted on Charles for a few days then revealed that she is going to visit her parents with their children.

"You'll be okay, won't you?" she asked.

Charles nodded, now too weak to put up an argument.

"Linda just got up and left," Orange said. "Here her husband was seriously ill and needed professional medical attention. But she took that as an opportunity to 'visit her parents.' This all was very strange."

Linda would leave the town of Hammond for four days. She would return but not go home immediately.

"Linda was a meticulous planner," Orange said. "She left the household with the full expectation that when she returned, Charles would be dead from the poison. Instead, she left town for four days and upon return realized that Charles was still alive. Determined to free herself of her ball and chain, she had to come up with a more direct plan."

Linda returned to the town of Hammond and rented out a motel room.

She told the older children to watch over the young ones and if they either left the motel or told anyone where she went that they would receive a spanking.

Linda then took the youngest child, Chuckie, with her and went to the gas station. She filled up two five-gallon cartons with gas.

She left Chuckie in the car as she pulled up in front of their home.

"She walked into that home like the Terminator," Orange said. "There was no subtlety to her actions whatsoever. She walked in determined to shoot her husband Charles to death."

She found the weakened Charles sleeping on his side in the bedroom. Linda wasted no time, firing one shot into his side. She then wrapped his body in a highly flammable garment bag.

Linda doused the bag with gas and kerosene.

She lit a match and toss it down on the body.

The entire room caught fire before the entire house exploded in flames, blowing out two walls.

Linda fled the scene of the crime with young Chuckie in tow.

THE AFTERMATH

Police and firefighters emerged on the scene almost immediately. Charles Darby's body was burned but not beyond recognition. Police then went searching for Linda and her missing children.

"Linda left behind volumes of evidence," Orange said. "She was identified by the service station attendant who remembered her pouring the gas into a carton instead of her vehicle. Tire tracks were discovered at the same which matched those of Linda's car. She took the rifle and hid it behind the vending machine at the motel where she stayed. She didn't go to great lengths to cover up her crime as again, it is my belief that she fully expected Charles to be dead from food poisoning when she returned home."

Linda had left the children behind at the motel and fled to the home of her parents. The police converged on her parent's home, dragging the wanted killer out of her mother's closet.

An autopsy on Charles' body would reveal large amounts of poison in his system.

"She was poisoning him over time," Orange said. "She thought she had finally done enough to kill him so she decided to leave town. When she would come back, she would let loose with some crocodile tears and act completely innocent."

At the murder trial, Linda's nine-year-old daughter Terri would take the stand. The young girl would testify that on the night of the murder her mother had entrusted her with the care of her younger siblings. Terri said that her mother gave her a stern warning before she left, stating that she would "whip" the girl if she told anyone that she had left and that she "wouldn't buy me anything else new."

"The most compelling evidence came from the daughter," Orange said. "She just left the children in the motel room, on their own, and then went to kill her husband in cold blood with a baby waiting out in the car. It was shocking then as it is now."

Linda's own defense attorney placed no witnesses on the stand. He instead focused on what he described as "rehearsed witnesses" and "tainted evidence."

The jury didn't buy his argument or Linda's innocence. They needed less than two hours to find Linda Darby guilty of first-degree murder.

SENTENCING AND ESCAPE

In October of 1970, Linda Darby was sentenced to life inside the Indiana State Women's Prison.

Two years later, however, Linda scaled the fence at the prison. Bloodied and scraped, she runs to her freedom.

She didn't plan out the escape. Linda was left alone, she saw the opportunity and she took it.

"She was under 'soft' surveillance," Orange said. "This really wasn't a high-security prison. Linda was placed in with low-level drug dealers and petty thieves. It took two years but she finally got fed up and wanted an escape. An out. That was Linda was all about. A woman who screwed up her life and others and sought escape only for herself."

Linda would later state that she ran away from prison because she believed that no one would ever found her innocent.

"I knew, you know, nobody would believe, you know, anything," Linda said. "Because every time while I was there, people came in and said I am innocent, I did not do it. That was the standard thing. And I got so I would not even say anything. Because I would think, well, they're lumping me with the rest of them."

She told a reporter that when she first escaped her first thought was to go and be with her children again. But then she realized that would be the first place the police would be waiting for her.

So she ran.

Her arms and legs bloodied, she sought refuge in a nearby house. It was there she met a man named Willy McElroy whom family members referred to as "Junior."

McElroy saw a sympathetic figure in Linda. She had told him that she had been beaten by her boyfriend and he immediately took her in with very little questions asked.

"Willy had the exact same psychological make-up as Charles Darby," Orange said. "Linda put for the damsel in distress routine and Willy fell for it just like Charles did. He saw himself as a hero. Only this time, Linda was desperate. She would tow the line now that she was a wanted fugitive. If that didn't inspire her to stop her escapes, nothing would."

A romance began between the two and they had a common-law marriage. No official certificates could be found between the two but Linda took on Willy's last name of McElroy.

Linda would give birth to two children with Willie.

FUGITIVE GRANDMOTHER
Flash forward thirty-five years later and Linda fully embraced her new identity as Linda McElroy.

House cleaner, wife, mother and now grandmother.

She continued to earn her living cleaning houses and caring for some of the elderly around the town of Pulaski, Tennessee. Her husband Willy had an antique shop and Linda would help out around the store, hobnobbing with the customers who milled around the store in the sleepy town of Pulaski.

Linda would have gotten away with her crime but for a new technology that emerged in 2007. Tennessee developed a system to "smoke out" escapees and Linda found herself targeted by the new software.

The software found similarities in Linda's name, social security and other data that was collected. There were other tip-offs which the agency refused to reveal but a key red flag was the fact that Darby never went to receive a driver license or state-issued identification.

"There is a part of me that thinks that someone ratted Linda out," Orange said. "Putting a variance under a social security number isn't enough to trip up a red flag. I think, at some point, someone got suspicious and started asking questions that she couldn't answer. Where did she come from? Where did she grow up? Especially when it came to Willy McElroy. You mean to tell me that this woman just popped up on your doorstep, battered and bloodied and you marry her with no questions asked? People can't be that stupid. Someone knew something and informed the authorities."

Within days of the implementation of the new tracking system, Linda came under the radar. She had spent over thirty-five years looking over her shoulder for the authorities to come calling. She had even befriended the town sheriff that came calling on her last day of freedom.

"Howdy Sheriff," Linda said with her usual cheer. "What can I do you for?"

"Linda," the sheriff said in a solemn tone. "Linda, I need to talk to you."

"What is it?" Linda said, stepping out of the door.

"I have a warrant."

"What's it about?"

"I need you to come to the station and talk to me."

Within 72 hours, Linda was returned to the same facility where she had scaled the fence thirty-five years earlier. Now, at sixty-eight years of age, she would not be scaling any other fences.

"Back in the day, we only had one side of the building fenced off," a prison spokesman said. "Now the entire perimeter is fenced in."

"I would love to know who killed Charles," Linda said during her one brief interview with the Nashville television station, WSMV. "I would love to know, and I would love to see them punished. But I didn't kill him."

Astonishingly, the local residents who knew Linda rallied around to show her support. A fund-raising campaign was bandied about but nothing came to fruition aside from on-line displays of support.

"She wouldn't hurt a flea," said Bill Hatfield who had known Darby for over twenty years. "She's cleaned our house for fifteen years and has a key to the house. I'd let her in tomorrow. She's never done anything but help people. She used to care for my elderly parents, staying at night from seven to seen and she had the full run of the house. She cared for my mother just like she was her own mother."

"We need to do something to show support," Elaine Jones said, a retired nurse who had known Darby for over thirty years. "I know she didn't do it, and somebody don't have that in them-this is a person I've known since the late 1970s-without getting in trouble or showing some signs of instability."

"But when do you stop?" Darby said when asked if she ever felt as if she were living a lie. "Where do you go back to?"

"I'm sorry," Linda said in a jailhouse interview. "I didn't mean to mislead anybody, but I didn't want to go back to something and pay for somebody else's crime. This is who I am. This is who I am. I'm not a murderer. I didn't do it."

"The community supported her after her arrest," Orange said. "They could not believe that she was capable of the crime she committed simply because she had kept her nose clean for the past thirty-five. Truth was, she had to stay low otherwise, she would have been sent back. Living clean for thirty-five years does not trump not paying for her murder. Charles Darby was an innocent man. A good man. He deserves justice."

"She deserves to be set free," an anonymous writer posted on a support site for Linda. "What happened in the past, happened. I don't see the point in sending the woman back to prison when she has been a decent citizen for the past thirty-five years."

"The amount of online support, both far and against was very interesting," Orange said. "Some people even suggested that everyone gets one "freebie" in life which would be amusing if it weren't so tragic. What Linda's supporters conveniently ignore is the fact that she killed an innocent man. If she had changed to the degree in which she had said she would have come clean and admitted wrong doing. Instead, she sought to escape as she always did in life. She escaped her first marriage by eloping with Charles then she escaped her obligations with Charles through murder. Then she escaped the crime by climbing over the barbed wire fence. Once she was caught again, she sought to escape through public appeal. Her supporters don't realize that they are enabling her in the same way her male paramours did only in their case, they won't wind up dead."

Linda Darby remains in the Indiana State Prison for Women.

TWISTED SISTERS : THE TRUE STORY OF REGINA AND MARGARET DEFRANCISCO

KORI MAYER

CHAPTER ONE

Regina and Margaret DeFrancisco are two sisters convicted of first degree murder.

On paper, the two sisters look like two girls you would see at a church social.

In school, both were good but not great students. Margaret was the pretty one. She would get all of the attention from the boys but return little interest.

Margaret was a student at Jones College Prep School, a selective public institution that is considered one of the top high schools in Illinois.

A little on the shy side, Margaret had a quick wit and sense of humor. Sweet-looking and pretty, she had avoided any kind of trouble throughout her young life. Her early photos suggest, however, that her subtle smirk was a couldn't contain the narcissism that was growing within.

"You would look at Margaret and see right through her," one of her neighbors said. "It was black, like was nothing there. She didn't seem like she had depth, like she had compassion."

Regina had a love for animals, particularly ponies. She rode horses and in her words, "never lost a show."

Regina was also the more extroverted of the two, wearing her emotions on her sleeve. She could mouth off and had a chip on her shoulder. She also had a thing for 'bad boys', seeing them as a reflection of herself.

"A lot of girls get turned on by the 'thug life'," forensic psychologist Marnie Clark said. "The DeFrancisco sisters definitely fit that mold. They were not out to play Mrs. Cleaver when they grew up. They were attracted to the gang lifestyle. They thought the drama was exciting."

The girls were raised by a single parent, Nora DeFrancisco. Nora raised the two sisters and their brother Joey in the Pilsen neighborhood of Chicago. Their father, Augie DeFrancisco was a small-time burglar and convicted drug dealer who had no involvement in the girl's childhood years. Their maternal grandfather, Gilbert Smith, was a former Chicago cop who was fired from the force in 1960 after admitting that he was "friendly with certain burglars."

Growing up in Pilsen, however, the girls could not avoid rubbing shoulders with gang members. They became enamored with gang culture, learning who fought against who and what the names of the gangs were. There were the Latin Counts, Kool Gang, Villa Lobos, Bishops, among many other offshoots. The girls knew what streets signified what gang members' territory and memorized their hand signals.

"Chicago is simply rife with gangs," Clark said. "It is inescapable, even to those in the more affluent communities. There is still a choice, however. For whatever reason, the DeFrancisco sisters were drawn to the 'thug life'. To a young person, it looks 'cool'. They are the classic examples of young women who could not see the big picture and thought the thug life was something worth aspiring to."

The two sisters, with their striking brunette looks, could not help but come into the cross hairs of the local gang members. They began wearing dark lipstick and teasing their hair out. Margaret would get a tattoo on her belly. Regina would have the letter "R" tattooed on her leg as well as a drawing of a heart just above her breast. They would hang out on street corners and in front of the local liquor store, chatting up the neighborhood 'gangstas'.

"The changes in their make-up and dress signified the changes in their personality," Clark said. "They grew bored during their time at prep school. Even ashamed. They did not want to see themselves as nerds and hated that aspect of themselves. Starting in eighth grade, it was time to start rebelling. By the time they reached high-school, the thug life was part of their persona. Dark make-up. Tattoos. Hanging out with gang bangers. Alcohol and drugs. But most important, they wanted all the drama that came with that kind of life. Who is out to get who, who dissed who and who shot who became their modus operandi in life."

Grandfather Gilbert, however, had seen this all before as a Chicago cop. He feared that the girls, particularly Regina, would become ensnared by the street gang culture. He tried to obstruct this from happening and found Regina a job with a local periodontist. He figured if he kept the girl busy with school and work it would keep her away from the idiots on the street.

Regina, however, did not have the emotional maturity to see the light. She showed up late for her first couple of shifts then she was fired.

But she had started dating a man named Johnny Rivera, a known member of Chicago's notorious "Latin Kings" street gang. Rivera had a rap sheet as long as "War and Peace" as well as more aliases than a Russian spy

Regina would learn how to package and deal drugs at the foot of Johnny. She would watch him put the cocaine into plastic bags, measuring it out by the ounce. They would drive around town and Johnny would introduce her to his customers, watching as he conducted the deals. The secret handshakes and secret lingo all became apart of Regina's world.

Officially crossing over from innocent prep school girl to drug dealing girlfriend, Regina lived a double life. She did manage to get a part-time job doing data entry work for a local law firm and had enrolled in the local junior college (Harold Washington).

Margaret was getting into trouble as well. Her grades in high school were slipping as she would sneak out at night to be with friends. She would often come to school looking "disheveled" according to one teacher who thought she looked like a child whose parents were going through a divorce.

And there was trouble on the home front.

Neighbors would report hearing the girls fighting with their mother on a daily basis.. The two girls were out of control with no father figure to put them in line. Nora would berate Regina whenever she would act up in school or get arrested and the girls would yell back.

In private, Nora would refer to her daughters as "the bitches".

Things would come to a head when Regina would get arrested for selling cocaine to an undercover cop. A single mom already strapped for cash as she had to support three children on her own, Nora was livid as she paid Regina's bail.

"How are you going to pay me back?" .

"I don't know!"

"Do you know how much it costs to bail you out of jail!" Nora screamed. "You are going to pay me back. You're going to pay me back every penny!"

CHAPTER TWO

"She needs money," Margaret said, her voice full of concern.

"How much?" Oscar asked.

"One thousand dollars. Can you help us out, baby?"

That was the scene set for the twenty-two year old Oscar Velazquez in June of 2000 as he spoke to the sister of his current teenage crush, Regina DeFrancisco. He spotted Regina around the neighborhood of Pilsen and quickly fell for her dark Irish-Italian good looks. Showing off his brand new Z28 Camaro, he chatted up the girls before he asked Regina out for tacos. The two began going out but Regina didn't like him...at first. Then she realized that he had some money and was all too willing to spend it on her.

"Oscar wasn't the typical guy that Regina would go for," Clark said. "Regina liked the 'bad boy', the thug. Oscar wasn't in street gang culture. He had immigrated from Mexico and actually had a real job, earning his living the old fashioned way as a truck driver. If anything, Regina would see someone like him as a sucker, someone who she could use."

Still, Regina was what Oscar wanted. He persisted in calling her, asking when he could see her again.

"He's a creepy guy," Regina told her sister, Margaret as her cell phone rang. She looked at the caller ID. Yep, it was Oscar.

"But maybe you can get some money from him?"

"Here, you talk to him," Regina said handing the cell phone to Margaret. "Just make up some baloney that I'm in jail or something."

"What?"

"Get rid of him. Tell him I need bail money."

"Hello, Oscar?" Margaret answered the phone.

"Yeah," Oscar said. "Who is this?"

"It's Margaret," she said, sounding as if she was trying to stifle tears. "Regina is in jail. She's locked up."

"What?"

"They put her in jail for something she didn't even do. They want one thousand dollars. One thousand dollars to bail her out."

Margaret smiled like a devil at her sister.

"I can help," Oscar said.

"No," Margaret said, sniffling. "It's too much."

"It's for your sister."

Oscar would persist in his willingness to help out, however. Margaret played him like a violin, agreeing to meet with Oscar to take his hard earned money.

"Oscar gave Margaret the money in the hopes of scoring points with the sisters," Clark said. "He thought that by being 'nice' and bailing them out of trouble they would find him attractive. Instead, it just fueled their contempt for him. These girls liked thugs. Bums. They cared little for Oscar's chivalry."

Regina would not use the money to pay back her mother, however. She would give the money to her real boyfriend, Johnny, who bought an "old school ride" car with Oscar's money.

Oscar would call Regina over twenty-four times during the next five days wanting to know what happened. He began to feel like the sucker he was.

He had a wife and kids in Mexico. But here in Chicago he fell for the brown-haired beauty and became all too willing to be her patsy.

"Oscar was playing with fire," Clark said. "He just didn't realize how far gone the girls were in terms of narcissism. He didn't see the fact that they didn't even see him as a human being. All he saw was batting eyelashes and pretty faces. He was totally smitten with Regina despite the fact that he had a wife and kids back in Mexico. Here he was, in Chicago, where he was free from the responsibilities of family. He could have a little fun and if he had to spend some money to do it, so be it."

CHAPTER THREE

The two sisters were surprised at how easy it was to extract money out of Oscar. With one fake phone call, they had one thousand dollars cash to their name.

"They were both attractive girls in the neighborhood," Clark said. "They were young, looking up to gang members and drug dealers for the power they had. But the girls realized that they had their own power. The power of budding sexuality that could make men do what they wanted. They could trick men into doing things for them with a future promise of sex."

Oscar continued to call and it would be only a matter of time before he would be confronted with the truth that he had been lied to. The girls had to construct a plan to get rid of him.

"I have an idea," Margaret said, picking up the cell phone and calling their fifteen year old friend, Veronica Garcia.

"Need your help," Margaret said as Veronica picked up.

"For what?" Veronica asked.

"I need a gun. Can you get a gun?"

"A gun?"

"Can your boyfriend get a gun?"

Veronica, like the DeFrancisco sisters, was enamored with street gang members. She had a boyfriend who could obtain whatever you needed, drugs or guns.

"Why?"

"We're going to stick up and rob Oscar," she said.

"You're not going to kill him are you?"

"We're just going to scare him a little," Margaret laughed.

Veronica did as she was asked, getting a gun from her boyfriend and heading straight over to the DeFrancisco sister's home.

"Nice," Margaret said, looking the pistol over, closing one eye as she looked through the cross hairs. "So where we going to do this?"

"Right here," Regina said, waving her hands around the living room.

"No way," Margaret said. "If the neighbors complain about us screaming and yelling then they're going to hear a gunshot. Duh."

Regina looked around the home. The basement door caught her eye.

"We'll lead him down there," Regina said, leading her sister down the basement steps. "Nobody can hear anything down here. The noise will be drowned out."

"Here," Margaret said, removing some blue tarp from the shelf. She spread the material down on the basement floor in front of the steps. "We can't leave any blood stains."

"Check you out," Regina laughed. "Miss Perry Mason."

Margaret laughed as she flattened out the tarp, placing it in a perfect line with the basement stairs. "Okay," she said, walking halfway up the steps. "So if we shoot him from here," pointing her forefinger into a gun. "He'll fall straight down there."

"Perfect."

The two sisters giggled and gave each other fist bump.

"Here is where the disconnect took place," Clark said. "They had embraced an environment and a culture where there were a lot of faux tough guys. Guys who said they would commit violence but for the most part it was all talk. The girls took it literally. At no point did they realize the gravity of what they were doing. They wanted to be 'gangstas', they wanted to be seen as 'hard'. They didn't have the maturity or the experience to realize that all of those 'gangstas' that they look up to are in jail. They didn't see Oscar at all. He was less than human. Something that is used, discarded and desecrated when it is no longer of use."

CHAPTER FOUR

Oscar was surprised that Regina finally called him back.

"Hey," she said, her teenaged voice soft and inviting.

"You're out of jail?" he asked.

"Yeah," she said. "I really appreciate what you did for me. That was really sweet of you."

"No worries," he said. "I need my money back. Been calling you like crazy."

"I'm sorry, I've just been busy."

"Yeah, I understand. But I need my money back."

"I was wondering if there was some other way I can pay you back?" she said in a sensual tone of voice.

"Like?"

"Like, I know you think my sister is hot, right?"

"What's that got to do with anything?"

"It is something we've been thinking about," she said. "But if you're not cool with it, it's okay."

"Not cool with what?"

"We were wondering if," Regina giggled. "If you can come over for a threesome."

Oscar couldn't believe his luck. He had heard of white girls being freaky, he just didn't think he would ever be able to experience it himself.

Naive to their plan, he rushed over and parked his car outside their mother's home in the South Side of Chicago.

He knocked on the door and was greeted by Margaret and Veronica Garcia, a friend of the two sisters. He didn't see the .38 caliber semi-automatic pistol had in her back waistband.

"Does anyone else know you're coming over?" Margaret asked.

"No," Oscar mumbled, shrugging his shoulder.

Margaret nodded her head and let the young man in. He saw Regina step into the room holding a bin of dirty laundry.

An awkward silence ensued followed by even more awkward smiles. The two sisters fed off each others willingness to go through with the plan. Even if one of them had second thoughts, they would be deemed "soft" by the other.

They had to go through with the murder.

Both women looked over at the young man with come hither looks. Regina said nothing as she opened the basement door and walked down.

"You go with Regina," Margaret said smiling.

"Right," Oscar said, his heart pounding in anticipation as he followed her down.

Oscar heard Margaret's footsteps behind him. What he didn't know was that she had a gun pointed at the back of his head.

When he reached the bottom step, she pulled the trigger.

The young man died instantly, falling face first in the tarp.

"Holy shit!" Margaret said. "I had no idea it would be that fucking loud. It doesn't sound that loud on TV."

Margaret came down the stairs. She kicked Oscar in the head hard, sending more blood spraying across the floor and wall.

"Nobody heard," Regina said as she knelt down and began rifling through Oscar's pockets.

"What the fuck was that?" Veronica said, calling down from the top of the basement steps.

"Did you see that? " Margaret asked. "He fell down like a baby!"

The sisters took out his wallet which had over $600 cash. They took his cell phone then ripped off the sterling silver chain from his neck.

"What the fuck happened?" Veronica said, her voice trembling as she came down a few steps.

"We shot his ass," Margaret said. "He's dead. Look at that shit, he's bleeding through his ears."

"Why did you do it?" Veronica screamed. "Why? Oh my God!"

"Shut the fuck up!" Margaret screamed.

"Don't just stand there," Regina commanded. "Come and help."

Their lifelong friend could only watch as the two sisters took out his car keys and wrapped up his body in a flowery bed sheet.

CHAPTER FIVE

"The girls suffered from what I call the 'Lord of the Flies' syndrome," Clark said. "Here they are hanging out with drug dealers, obtaining guns, killing men in the basement. There is no parental figure in sight! They are left to fend for themselves and the end result is murder and mayhem."

With the dead body in the basement, both sisters peeked out their window, waiting for dark.

Confident that the entire neighborhood was asleep, they opened the door and carried Oscar's body out of the home.

The three girls struggled carrying the dead weight, wrapping his body with a comforter and the flowered bed sheet.

They opened up the trunk and placed the body inside.

"What are you guys doing?" a woman yelled from a window across the street.

The girls looked up startled.

"We're getting rid of some furniture" Regina called out. "No worries."

The girls waved at the neighbor as she moved away from the window.

"Nosy bitch," Regina whispered.

Margaret giggled. Veronica still scared, said nothing.

They got into the vehicle and drove to a vacant lot where they took out Oscar's body again.

"This is hard work," Regina complained. "Shit!"

They plopped the body on the ground, looking at it for a beat before Regina reached back into the trunk. She pulled out a bottle of nail polish remover and poured the liquid over the tarp.

"Are you sure that's gonna work?" Margaret asked.

"It says 'highly flammable,'" Regina said, shrugging her shoulders.

Margaret lit a match and set the material on fire.

The flame went up immediately, the girls could feel the warmth on their faces in the cold Chicago night.

"Told you this shit would work!" Regina said.

Then as fast as the flame started, it quickly died down.

"Light another one," Regina said.

Margaret threw down another match, getting the flames going again as Regina doused the tarp with the remaining nail polish remover.

Satisfied, the girls quickly got back into the Camaro and drove off.

******

An anonymous call came into police headquarters reporting the fire in the vacant lot. The caller investigated further, however, and saw Oscar's arm sticking out through the fire. He called 911 again with a sense of urgency, telling them of the body.

CHAPTER SIX

When police on scene identified Oscar Velazquez' partially burned body, their initial knee-jerk reaction was that this was the work of a local street gang, a drug deal gone awry. But when they found the nail polish remover bottle, however, they quickly realized that this was the work of amateurs. A jealous girlfriend maybe.

Meanwhile, the DeFrancisco sisters cruised around town over the following days, trying to pawn off the Camaro.

"This is where the sisters make the guys in 'Dumb and Dumber' look like geniuses," Clark said. "They had only pre-planned the front end of the murder. Like most impulsive killers, they had no idea what to do after. Their greed took over and they decide to sell the Camaro. They have no papers for it, duh, and really can only sell a stolen vehicle to a thug. They find no takers as even the dumbest street gang member isn't going to buy a hot car from two teenaged girls. So they cruise around town and Oscar's brother spots them in the car."

The girls, failing in their sales efforts, would later abandon he vehicle behind a storefront and set it on fire.

**

The day after Oscar's killing, a mutual friend named Jessica Benitez stopped by the house. Jessica went downstairs and watched Margaret mop up a stain of blood near the basement steps.

"The hell is that?" she asked.

Margaret said nothing as she poured bleach over the blood, scrubbing hard.

"Dude bled all over the floor," Regina said. "But only after Margaret kicked him in the head. We called him over, told this idiot we'd have a threesome with him. Then we robbed his ass."

"But the blood stain on the floor-" Jessica asked, watching Margaret clean up.

"We killed a guy," Margaret said without remorse.

"He was going to kill us!" Regina said. "Margaret shot him in the back of the head. We searched his body and found a gun in his waistband. Then we wrapped him up in plastic and put him in his car."

"Holy shit, girl," Jessica.

"We're about to go on the run," Margaret announced.

"Aren't you scared?" Jessica asked, looking back down at the blood stain in the basement.

"I ain't scared of nothing," Margaret said. "You should have seen his head when I shot him. His brain oozed out like cheese."

Margaret made a rolling motion with her hands.

Jessica then accompanied Margaret to the store she purchased a bottle of blonde hair dye for her "disguise."

"We see here how the whole street gang culture has influenced the behavior of these girls," Clark said. "At any point in time, Veronica or Jessica could have went straight to the police. But they get caught up in the drama of the moment. The so-called 'loyalty' to their friend who, quite frankly, would shoot them up in a heartbeat if they knew that they were going to be a snitch."

Going off the tip from Oscar's brother, the police show up to question both Regina and Margaret. The duo denied ever seeing Oscar.

They then go to interview Veronica Garcia.

They found the jittery fifteen year old to be a different story, however. The teen quickly crumbled under the pressure of questioning and told the police the entire story.

Feeling the heat, the DeFrancisco sisters go on the run...

CHAPTER SEVEN

For all of their stupidity in committing the murder, the DeFrancisco sisters deftly avoided capture for almost two years.

They decided to split up. Margaret would go to live with their maternal aunt in Roscoe, Illinois, an hour and a half drive away from where they lived. Roscoe was a small town with less then 10,000 people, a far cry from the drug infested streets of Chicago. Margaret's worst dreams were now realized. She was now a nerd who had to stay inside all day long, living in a boring cul-de-sac with no street gang action. Neighbors would remark that they would never see her and if hey did she would quickly go back inside.

Living underground without detection, it took a broadcast of the television show AMERICA'S MOST WANTED to generate an anonymous tip which led to Margaret's whereabouts. Police staked out her aunt's apartment and entered, finding Margaret in her bedroom with a blank look on her face.

"My feelings were hurt bad because she (my wife) did something behind my back," Margaret's uncle by marriage said later. "I knew (police) were going to find her anyway."

Seven months later, Regina was captured in Dallas living with her Latin King boyfriend, Johnny Rivera.

Initially, she did not even know where the gang banger lived. She just knew the town, Laredo, and she journeyed there by bus. Regina would eventually find him, locating one of his relatives. She would live under an alias and claimed that she worked as a maid.

Police knew better. Regina made money by selling drugs under the Latin King banner.

Unlike Margaret, Regina had evaded the scrutiny of the America's Most Wanted viewers.

Her capture came about because she could not stop hanging out with the wrong crowd.

Two sheriffs were had mistakenly arrived at her boyfriend's apartment, wanting to serve a warrant to someone else.

Rivera allowed the deputies to enter his apartment but he had left a marijuana flake on his table. Police searched the apartment further and found several packages of crack cocaine ready to be sold.

The deputies arrested Rivera. They searched inside the apartment and interviewed Regina, who was groggy from a cocaine high. She showed them her false Texas identification and they let her go.

But the deputies smelled something fishy on her aside from marijuana. They had the apartment manager set up a meeting with her. She arrived at the complex in an SUV with another man. The police approached and the SUV sped away.

The high-speed chase down residential Dallas streets reached upwards of 90 mph. The SUV then slammed into a center median, the front tires blowing out.

Regina got out of the car and tried to sprint away. A deputy tackled her and they fell to the ground, her cell phone skidding across the gravel road. Sifting through her pockets, the officer found over $1,500 cash.

She was taken to Dallas County Jail where they discovered her true identity.

"We pulled her out of jail," said a Deputy Dodson. "I asked to see one of her tattoos, and she showed me...I called her by name, but she never said a word to me. She knew it was over."

She was then extradited to Illinois to stand trial for the murder of Oscar Velazquez.

CHAPTER EIGHT

The trial of the two women began in July of 2004 and both sisters pleaded not guilty by reason of self-defense.

But their friend, Veronica Garcia, had cut a deal with prosecutors in return for a lesser sentence. She would provide the testimony that would damn the two sisters to prison.

Garcia said that she didn't know what the sisters had planned. She had simply provided the gun to the DeFrancisco's which she thought would be used for a robbery only.

"I didn't see her shoot Oscar," Veronica said.

The prosecution brought forth additional witnesses in Jessica Benitez, Luciana Macias, and Maria Constantino, the neighbor.

"Both of them told me that they killed Oscar," Jessica said. "Margaret kicked him in the head so he could die faster."

"I saw them load the body into the back of the Camaro," Constantino said. "Regina told me that she planned out the killing."

Margaret, however, maintained their innocence. She said that Oscar came to the apartment angry because the sisters had tricked him out of one-thousand dollars.

"I shot him to protect Regina," Margaret said.

"Then why didn't you tell the reporting officer what happened?" the prosecution attorney asked.

"We would've got in trouble," Margaret said. "If I told the truth, I would've been there longer."

Regina DeFrancisco would also take the stand and claim self-defense as well.

"I came out of my bedroom," Regina said. "And he was there, cursing and screaming. He pulled a gun on me. I thought I was going to die. I curled up on the floor, in a fetal position. I begged for my life. Then I heard a gunshot and saw Margaret standing over Oscar, holding a gun."

"Whose idea was it to dispose of the body?"

"Veronica knew of this vacant lot," Regina said. "It was her idea."

The jury would deliberate for over six and a half hours. Regina would be found guilty of murder. Margaret's jury, however, was unable to convict her. There was and 11 to 1 deadlock with one juror believing that she should be acquitted. The juror did not believe that someone so young could commit murder.

Margaret was then released from custody and told to await retrial. She had a baby during this time, a girl, and would find work as a nursing assistant while she awaited another trial.

Four months later, Margaret would be given another day in court. Veronica Garcia would once again be the star witness for the prosecution, detailing the exact same testimony as before.

There would be no deadlock in this second go around as Margaret would be convicted of first-degree murder.

Regina would be sentenced to 35 years in prison while Margaret would be sentenced to 46 years. Both women are now jailed at the Dwight Correctional Center. They have each filed appeals which have been denied.

"The girls cared nothing about Oscar Velazquez," Clark said. "In the end, they remained true to their own narcissistic nature. They only cared about what was happening to the next. They cared about nothing about the now fatherless children Oscar Velazquez would leave behind nor about the fact that the took his life."

Veronica Garcia was jailed for five years. She served her full sentence and has since been released.

"This is a cautionary tale if there ever was one," Clark said. "The sisters had it all. They had access to one of the finest schools in their state. Yet they chose to throw it all away for short money and the cheap thrill of the 'thug life.' In the end, they got to see what the 'thug life' was really all about. Mindless violence where everyone is out for themselves, especially when there is a plea bargain to be made. They could have had it all had they stayed on the straight and narrow. Now they have nothing."

KILLER NURSE BEVERLY ALLITT

JENNIFER PARRIS

Beverly Allitt-the Angel of Death

It is hard to believe that a young female could be capable of murder, let alone multiple murders. It is even more shocking that a female nurse could carry out such terrible crimes. That is exactly what Beverly Allitt did though. This nurse is Britain's most infamous female serial killer and also goes by the name of the Angel of Death due to her responsibility to care for others but instead used her nursing position to kill people. Over a short period of fifty-nine days in her job as a nurse in a children's ward, she killed four young children and attempted to kill at least nine others either by causing cardiac arrest or hypoglycemia. The Angel of Death did not appear to be an evil killer though. She was very well mannered with parents, which is how she gained their trust with their precious loved ones. But after similar/suspicious causes of death in the children's ward, investigations at the hospital showed missing nursing records and the presence of Allitt with every one of those cases.

Childhood

As a child, Beverly Allitt liked attention and would go about negative ways of getting it. She was born in October of 1968 and was one of four children (two sisters and one brother). Her father worked in an off-licence (a British shop where the liquor is sold off premises) and her mother cleaned schools. Neighbors described Allitt as affectionate because she liked to volunteer and often would babysit. She did her chores at home and saved the money she earned. Teachers also really liked her and was considered one of their favorites. She went to school at Charles Read Secondary Modern School because she failed the exam needed to attend Kesteven and Grantham Girls' School.

She often would wear casts and bandages as a kid without letting her injuries be examined. She got worse as she got older and became overweight. During this time in her life, she was sick and injured more frequently. She often engaged in self-injury and spent a lot of time in and out of various hospitals due to different ailments such as gall bladder pain, back trouble, ulcers, headaches, and blurred vision, just to name a few. Her reasons were that she had been hit on her bike by a passing car or had fallen off a horse or even had been burned. Most of her problems were either made up or self-inflicted. She convinced a doctor to take out her healthy appendix. Then, she constantly interfered with the scar to keep it from healing. Another time, she stabbed herself in the hospital with the intention of injecting her body with water. Next, there was the time when she tampered with a thermometer in the hospital. Because she was physically healthy, she had to see lots of different doctors in order to keep them treating her.

Allitt was a frequent liar and not just about her illnesses. She would often make up stories. One time, she told people that her parents had split up and that she would have to go live with her aunt. The tales would be investigated and found out to not be true.

Beverly Allitt dreamed of becoming a nurse and attended school at Grantham College and began her studies at the age of sixteen. During her last year of school, she was absent approximately one hundred and twenty-six days with numerous illnesses. Nurses there also described her as odd. There were some at the school that thought Allitt would benefit from psychiatric help.

She did manage to find a boyfriend at Grantham College really only because she forced Stephen Biggs to be hers. He bought her a ring but she never set a date for the wedding and refused to hold his hand in public. Once, she faked a pregnancy. She said that Stephen had AIDS. Another time, she lied about being raped by a former boyfriend. Allitt was described as deceptive by her boyfriend.

Eventually, Allitt's odd injuries (real or fake) were thought to be from a controversial personality disorder known as Munchausen Syndrome. People with this disorder like to be ill because of the attention they get from others when they are sick as well as the satisfaction of fooling doctors with their self-inflicted illnesses and injuries. They often have long medical histories. They are frequent liars and have lab tests that lead to no answers for the doctors to diagnose a patient. Allitt may have liked the attention because even though her childhood seemed to be relatively normal, there could have been emotional needs that were not being met.

Nursing Career

Beverly Allitt went on to become a nurse but the odd behavior from her childhood still continued. She took her nursing exams and actually failed them because she was absent quite often due to her various illnesses.

After that, Allitt managed to find a job at a nursing home. Like at school, she was gone quite often. Once, when she was there, it was thought that she smeared feces on the walls.

In 1991, at the age of twenty-three, Beverly Allitt surprisingly got a six-month contract job at Grantham and Kesteven Hospital that is located in Lincolnshire working in the children's ward. This ward was for newborn babies up to the age of sixteen. Kids sent to this hospital often had minor illnesses. They were quickly treated and then sent home as soon as they were well.

When Allitt arrived at the hospital, she had had less than two years of experience at this point and was not even a qualified children's nurse. It was shocking that she even was considered for a job considering how many days of class she missed when attending nursing school. The only reason she got the job was because the hospital was understaffed and no one else applied for the job. At the time, there were only two day nurses and one night nurse. According to one of those nurses, Mary Reet, who worked at the hospital at the same time as Allitt, "There was something about her that I didn't like but couldn't pinpoint it" (Birmingham Mail). She thought that she seemed cheerful, friendly, and helpful, however. Allitt was even respected. She was the one calling the alarms and identifying problems that the very sick children were experiencing.

Because of her job working with others, it meant that she was no longer getting personal attention but it allowed her to find attention in other ways that were just as negative as when she was a kid. The nurse was able to use this opportunity to get close to the patients. Allitt was able to befriend all of her patients' parents by suggesting that they leave to go get some coffee. Through this recommendation, the parents were trusting her and allowing her to be alone to administer treatment to the children. The parents had really appreciated the nurse at the time because of her actions during this difficult time when their children were sick. It was her care and love for her patients that caused the parents to call her an angel. She would even ride with the patients in the ambulance if they needed to be transferred to another hospital. However, Allitt was far from an angel. The term *Angel of Death* is given to medical professionals that are supposed to be healing patients but are really causing them harm.

The angel changed a week after she arrived at the hospital and odd things began to happen. Money was being stolen from the nurses. A key to the insulin refrigerator had disappeared. This is also when the young patients began experiencing odd symptoms that were very serious. Some of the patients died. At Grantham and Kesteven Hospital, usually only one child died a year. Once Allitt started working, four children died in just a period of a few months.

The Victims

Allitt's reign of terror began on February 21, 1991. Though it is not exactly clear how many children she actually did harm, the definite numbers are four murders and nine that were purposely harmed all within a fifty-nine-day time period. The ages of her patients were between seventeen weeks to eleven years old.

Seven-month-old Liam Taylor was Beverly Allitt's first victim. He had a chest infection and had come to the hospital for treatment. Since Allitt was able to befriend the parents, they left the hospital to get some rest. Once they returned, they learned from her that Liam had experienced respiratory problems but had recovered. She tried to convince the parents to leave again but they chose to stay. He suffered more respiratory problems under Allitt. She let the emergency team at the hospital know once he started becoming pale. The other nurses on the floor were confused because no alarms sounded when he had stopped breathing. He did survive but he had suffered cardiac arrest and brain damage. He was put on life support and was later taken off of it by his parents. His death at the time was ruled as heart failure.

Timothy Hardwick was Allitt's next victim. He was the oldest victim at eleven. He had cerebral palsy and dealt with seizures. The emergency team was notified when the boy turned blue and had no pulse. Allitt stood by as the defibrillator was used. Unfortunately, the boy died. There was an autopsy performed but there were no answers to the cause of his death. Epilepsy was eventually ruled as the cause.

The third victim was one-year-old Kayley Desmond. She had a chest infection but was getting better. After being in the care of Allitt though, she went into cardiac arrest. She was revived and transferred to another hospital. Once there, doctors discovered that there was a puncture hole under her armpit and also an air bubble. It was decided that it was probably due to an accidental injection. Because Kayley was transferred to the other hospital, she did survive.

Allitt's next victim was five-month-old Paul Crampton. He had been admitted for a minor infection. The nurse was not actually on duty when he was admitted but after she took over, Paul's condition deteriorated. He experienced an episode of insulin shock and nearly went into a coma. The Angel of Death was the one that raised the alarm about his serious condition. Doctors were very confused about the changes in insulin levels. After a few days, Paul began to feel better and Allitt was asked by the doctor to remove his drip. Shortly after that, he became quite ill for the second time. When he started feeling better, the dad decided to take a short break from the hospital room. The nurse was once again left in charge and the baby suffered the third attack. He was transferred to another hospital. Allitt actually went with him in the ambulance. She was also the one that had suggested that the doctors test the baby's blood sugar. Thankfully, Paul survived at the other hospital. After a few weeks, his test results came back. He had actually had 43,147 milliunits of insulin in his blood. That is one of the highest levels found in a human. The only other person that had levels this high died. It was a wonder that Paul survived with Allitt as his nurse.

Next on Allitt's list was Bradley Gibson at five years old. He had pneumonia and under the care of the Angel of Death, went into cardiac arrest. It was discovered that he also had high insulin. That night, he had a heart attack but was transferred to a second hospital and was able to survive.

Yik Hung Chan was two when he came to the hospital to recover from a fractured skull from a fall. He ended up turning blue while Allitt was working. He was given oxygen, transferred to another hospital, and recovered. The nurse was not blamed though because it was thought that the fracture was behind the boy's symptoms.

Next, Beverly focused her attention on twins on two different occasions. The twins were born premature and were under her supervision. The first twin, Becky, was found to have been cold and hypoglycemic but was released that evening. Then, that night, Becky woke up in pain but a doctor just said it was colic. She died that night. That is why the second twin, Katie, came back to the hospital for observation. Katie stopped breathing a couple of times while there. Her lungs collapsed and she suffered from brain damage and was transferred to another hospital. There, it was also discovered that five of her ribs had been broken but surprisingly, she lived. Her parents were so happy that they asked Allitt to be Katie's godmother. She agreed despite Katie having to live with partial paralysis, sight and hearing damage, and cerebral palsy.

After this, there were four additional victims that also suffered from similar symptoms as the other patients over a short period of fifteen days. There was seven-year-old Michael Davidson, nine-month-old Christopher King, eight-month-old Christopher Peasgood, and seven-week-old Patrick Elstone. Patrick was oxygen deprived and became brain damaged. People were starting to get suspicious about what was going on at this hospital.

Finally, Claire Peck, age fifteen months, became Allitt's last victim. This little baby had asthma and required a breathing tube. She was only under the care of the nurse for a couple of minutes when she had a heart attack. She survived but then had a second one later, leading to her death. It was thought that her death was because of natural causes. It was later found that she had been injected with lignocaine. This drug is not administered to babies. Claire was the Angel of Death's last victim after fifty-nine days of work.

The Investigation

After the numerous number of cardiac cases in the last few months at Grantham and Kesteven Hospital, an inquiry was launched into the cause of all of them. Deaths and comas at children's hospitals are actually pretty rare; especially if they are unexplained. At this particular children's hospital, usually only one child died a year. At first, it was thought that maybe there was a virus in the air that was making the patients sicker than when they arrived. This turned out to be incorrect. The nurses on the floor, including Beverly Allitt, talked about how maybe there was a parent or some outsider sneaking in and causing harm. That was when security cameras were placed in the hospital and the staff became more careful. They were also being watched by other people that worked in the hospital.

Next, it was discovered that there was a lot of potassium in Claire's blood. The police were called into the investigation and realized that there was lignocaine in Claire's system. This drug is given to people during cardiac arrest but is never given to a baby.

It was then that the police began to suspect that all the deaths were probably not due to natural causes. In fact, there were a lot of victims that had had high levels of insulin. To figure out what was going on, the police had a secret meeting with the hospital management to talk about a possible killer. After that, information came about that Allitt had actually reported that the key to the refrigerator where the insulin was stored had gone missing.

The next thing to do was check the daily nursing logs. Coincidentally, they were missing. The pages for the time of Paul Crampton's visit had been torn out of the book. There was also another record book that was gone. The pages were actually discovered at Allitt's house. The missing records along with her presence at every incident involving the mysteriously ill children led to her arrest.

Mary Reet, one of Allitt's coworkers was actually stunned at first to hear of her arrest. She was sure that the police had made a mistake. In fact, Katie's parents wanted to protect their daughter's godmother.

They hired a detective to help prove her innocence. They even let the nurse continue to babysit Katie. Other people in the United Kingdom were also shocked. There had never been a nurse that had killed patients in the country. But with the evidence that had been collected, there was definitely no mistake about who was guilty of harming thirteen or more innocent hospital patients that were all so very young.

The Arrest/Trial

The police thought that they had enough evidence to convict Allitt but she was not actually charged until several months later. When interrogated, she did not seem scared about talking to the police. She denied any wrongdoing and said that all she had been doing was caring for the ill children. She even claimed that she was not at the hospital on some of the days in question and that at the other times she had come on the scene later and that she had been trying to help like a good nurse would do. At that point, the police did not have enough evidence to convict her so they had to let her go for the time being but that still did not erase their suspicions and she was suspended from the hospital. After all, the events at the hospital were certainly suspicious. Also, the other nurses said that she never liked to pick up crying babies and that she never seemed saddened by the deaths of any of the children. Later, she was eventually arrested.

With the investigation of Allitt's Munchausen Syndrome that led her to desire attention through the suffering of various medical conditions, it was also found that she dealt with Munchausen Syndrome by Proxy. This personality disorder is very similar to Munchausen Syndrome but instead of making oneself ill, the individual makes another one ill in order to get attention. People with Munchausen Syndrome sometimes also have Munchausen Syndrome by Proxy like Allitt. In Beverly situation, when the nurse found that she was no longer getting attention for her own medical disorders, she switched to causing them because she was able to receive attention from parents and other nurses by acting like the hero for the victims when she cared for them. The victims of people with Munchausen Syndrome by Proxy are usually children because they are unable to speak up for themselves. Allitt was made out to look like a hero at times while still working at the hospital because she was caring for the children that had become seriously ill. She was even able to diagnose some of the children's ailments rather than the doctors since she had caused the illnesses. Such as in the case of Katie, the twin, Allitt was made godmother which gave her the attention she craved.

Despite her love of attention, she did not want the attention for being a criminal. She wanted what she thought was positive attention in which people pitied her since she was sick quite often.

Allitt was evaluated by medical professionals for her disorders while in jail but she never did confess to the crimes. While she was awaiting trial however, Allitt lost a ton of weight which developed into anorexia. This was just another example of the psychological problems she experienced. Because of all of her past (and now present) illnesses, she repeated her absenteeism from nursing school and only attended sixteen days of the two-month long trial.

The trial was difficult because even though the evidence pointed to her, there were no fingerprints or any eyewitnesses. Everything was circumstantial. It had taken nearly nine months to gather the evidence that had been presented in court. The police were definitely worried about what the jury would decide. The jury deliberated for six days before they made the big decision about the Angel of Death.

She was eventually charged with four counts of murder, eleven counts of attempted murder, as well as eleven counts of causing serious harm to her patients. The parents of the victims, including the police, were overjoyed with the verdict. Justice would be served for what she had done to their children. The nurse was then given thirteen life sentences in 1993 for the murder and attempted murder of the innocent children that became her victims. Munchausen Syndrome by Proxy had no impact on the judge's decision of the extremely severe sentence that was given to Allitt. This is actually the harshest punishment ever given to a female. The judge said that he recommended that she spend at least forty years in prison before parole would even be considered but it became thirty years. As the judge said when she was sentenced, "You have turned the hospital where you worked into a killing field" (Birmingham Mail).

Allitt will be 54 in 2022 when the thirty-year possible parole could even become a possibility. It will only happen though if she has become a reformed person and is no longer a danger to herself or to anyone else. It does not change that she is still a murderer, despite having the label of Munchausen Syndrome or Munchausen Syndrome by Proxy. Though it does not seem likely that she will be released, the parents of the victims say that no matter what, they will fight back if there ever comes a chance of her leaving the prison/hospital where she is serving her time.

Prison

Allitt was sent to Rampton Secure Hospital in Nottingham to serve her sentence under the Mental Health Act. This hospital is a facility that has high security to protect prisoners suffering from mental disorders. It is not a prison because the patients/prisoners are there to receive treatment. Chris Taylor, the father of Liam Taylor, was not pleased with her placement. He thought she should be sent to jail and that it would not matter whether she killed herself in prison or not. She was sent to the hospital by the judge because of her history of self-harm. Taylor, however, looks at it as a place to take a vacation because she has a TV and is allowed to talk to other people at the hospital to form relationships with them. There is a bar and the hospital throws discos. Occasionally, Allitt has even been allowed to go out shopping as long as she is with a guard. During an interview, the former nurse mentioned that she liked the place because of the freedom it gave her that she would not receive in jail. In order for prisoners like Beverly Allitt to enjoy the freedom while receiving treatment, it costs the taxpayers of the United Kingdom £2000 a week for each inmate to stay there.2000

Her problems with Munchausen Syndrome have not ended despite being at Rampton Secure Hospital in order to receive her treatment. Once she arrived, she ate glass, stabbed herself with paperclips, and poured boiling water on her hands. On the plus side, she did admit to three of the murders and to six of the attempted ones.

Beverley was a young nurse that should have had the desire to help young children and be an advocate and a voice for them in order to heal. Growing up, she craved attention and went about negative ways to get it. She would either purposely hurt herself or lie about being ill in order to get attention. Things did not get better as she got older. Instead, she took advantage of her position at the hospital where she worked as a children's nurse. She harmed and killed many children so that she could get attention for herself. Through her attention desiring ways, she killed four children and hurt at least eleven more in the fifty-nine days that she worked as a children's nurse. Parents trusted the woman that later would become known as the Angel of Death. She will no longer be able to hurt another patient or child anymore since she has been given thirteen life sentences and will unable to be eligible for parole for at least thirty years (and that is only if she is able to show that she is no longer a danger to society).

GWEN HENDRICKS

DORA ENGLISH

Gwen Gillespie Hendricks was born into a Navy family in Memphis, Tennessee in 1955.

Her father was a naval officer while her mother was a housewife. Like most military families, they moved often from station to station, according to her father's assignment. Growing up in a devoutly Catholic home and Gwen would embrace the religion with fervor.

Gwen dressed with modesty, wearing button down shirts and minimal make-up. She fostered a nerd look, with wire-rimmed glasses and short hair.

Carrying on the family's military tradition, she joined the Air Force at the age of twenty-five. It was there she would meet Jim Hendricks, twenty-four, who was her instructor.

Jim Hendricks was a tall, strapping Air Force sergeant with an air of authority. He had an easy smile and Gwen found him easy on the eyes.

"Well, it was kind of instant attraction," Gwen recalled. "There was a bit of lust there as he's a very tall, handsome man. The Air Force can tell you that you can't date but they can't tell you who to marry so I went to the Jag office and asked if I could marry my STA and they said 'yes.'"

The two were married in 1980. Jim had a five year old daughter, Season Hendricks, from a previous relationship. In 1982, they would have a son, Ben.

Because of their career choice, the couple spent a lot of time apart during the early years of their marriage. Jim was stationed at Wake Island while Gwen was assigned to Eglin Air Force Base in Florida.

The couple would be reunited in 1986 as Jim was assigned to the Air Force Academy in Colorado Springs. Gwen would not re-enlist in the Air Force, instead taking a job with the Internal Revenue Service.

The couple spent three years in Colorado before Jim would be transferred to Guam in August of 1989. He took the the entire family with him to the island.

"I figured we had a pretty normal family," Season said. "Until we moved to Guam. Things started to change. She (Gwen) would pick fights. She was jealous of the time my Dad and I would spend together."

"She (Gwen) had a different life in mind for herself," forensic psychologist Joyce Smith said. "She was used to having her own money. So when they moved to Guam there was little to do and less money to do it with."

Gwen and the children moved back to the United States, returning to Colorado and leaving Jim in Guam.

She would buy a home in Littleton and once again start working for the IRS. She then joined the junior Chamber of Commerce where she met Terry Knaack and a woman named Rochelle.

"Rochelle was into tarot cards," Gwen said. "And Terry was into new age occultism. My religion, my faith was still very meaningful to me. I wanted to do Bible study with them to get them out of what I considered witchcraft. Rochelle said she wouldn't go to Bible study with me unless I did the cards with her and the same with Terry. So I think I opened up the door to hell. Right after I started, everything went wrong"

During this time, Gwen began to experience health issues. She suffered from dizzy spells and nausea.

Her personality shifted as well, changing from being even-tempered to easily agitated and manic. With her health and ability to focus effected, Gwen stepped down from her revenue collector position to tax examiner.

"Could the illness have played a part in her deciding to kill her husband?" Smith asked. "Maybe. But Gwen was really steeped into religion and sounded like she embraced some of the more fringe elements of Christianity. She truly believed that occultism was a form of witchcraft and that those things could do her harm. So when she suffered from her illness she erroneously attributed it to her dabbling in the occult. She was a woman who preferred supernatural explanations to rational thought."

Gwen also started to grow deeper into debt, buying expensive gifts for friends.

In the fall of 1990, Gwen hired Terry Knaack to help remodel the Littleton home. A few months later, Knaack moved into the couple's basement with the rationale being he would be able to help with the mortgage. With the husband away and a man in the home, Gwen began to fantasize about Terry and starting over with him.

"Terry would talk a lot about wanting to having a ranch for children with special needs," Gwen recalled. "And I started having delusions that he and I would start this ranch together for the children."

"She entered into a fantasy world," Smith said. "She began imagining a life with this other man, having delusions of grandeur of what they would do together. He became her willing accomplice in her dreams, since her own husband was absent because of military duty. So an alternate universe with Terry Knaack became her obsession. What probably started as harmless day dreams soon grew into something sinister."

"I also believe that Gwen had more than a little bit of a Messiah complex. She had this compulsion to save people and it manifested in doling out gifts and handouts to people who she felt were in need. She had this secret life and kept things from Jim who was away on military assignment. Those secrets involved getting into credit card debt."

By January of 1991, Gwen began telling friends that she was having premonitions of Jim dying in a plane crash.

"I had this really bad dream over and over again," Gwen recalled. "Where Jim had died in a plane crash. I was thinking, well after Jim died that I would marry Terry and we'd start this ranch but of course Terry didn't know anything about because it was all in my head."

Gwen then began hearing voices.

"They (the voices) wanted me to sacrifice what was most dear in my life," Gwen recalled. "I remember thinking that I have to answer these voices because this is coming from God. You know, I've got to sacrifice what I loved the most and that was Jim."

Gwen kept a journal where she logged the "premonitions" of her husband's death. She titled the journal "The Courage to Will and Persevere," She described the voices that she heard and believed that God had told her to kill Jim.

"She experienced what we call 'command hallucinations,'" said Smith. "These are sometimes coupled with someone's value system, in this case, it was Gwen's religion. Gwen believed that she should obey God and believed that the voices that she heard were, in fact, coming from God. So this could go bad real quick if those voices told her to do damage to someone."

"She was past the breaking point, a delusional schizophrenic that was not diagnosed. When she confided with friends it was probably with people who shared her same point of view, people who believed in visions, messages from God and premonitions. Gwen was a soft-spoken woman and even if someone thought she was crazy they would not think she would be capable of taking a gun and blowing someone's brains out. She didn't have that violent vibe."

But behind closed doors, Gwen would deal with problems or difficulties in a haphazard fashion. She would often open up the Bible and believed that whatever random verse she came upon was a direct message from God.

"I reread Psalm 90 quite a few times before a small voice said, 'Keep reading, keep reading.'" Gwen wrote in her journal. "After reading the first page of stanzas, I knew I would be protected from the car bombs, the knifings, the guns, the contracts and all the other evil I had seen connected with busting the pornographers and pimps. Those mafia guys play rough, but somehow they just won't be able to get me. Then I turned the page to continue reading. It felt like a giant fist had slammed into my heart. I literally could not breath [sic]. I burst into sobs and sunk to the floor. I cried for Jim because he really was going to die."

Gwen began to prepare for Jim's death, taking out a $300,000 life insurance policy on her husband payable on his death.

She then visited a local banker, informing him that she would be soon be receiving proceeds from insurance claim. Gwen was told that she would not be able to use the money as long as Jim was alive. She then forged a doctor's note which alleged that she had multiple sclerosis. She submitted this note to the Red Cross along with a letter stating that they should be responsible for being her husband back from Guam.

Gwen did not want the proceeds from the insurance for her own material gain. She believed that she could use the proceeds from his life insurance to establish the "James Hendricks Foundation" to aid victims of mafia produced pornography.

"She became obsessed with pornographers," Smith said. "Like most people with Messiah Complexes, she chose an ill of society and focused on that, believing that she was a chosen vessel to help eradicate the 'sin'. In her deluded mind, she needed this money to accommodate God's will to establish this ranch wherein she would save victims of pornography. The only way she could attain this goal would be to kill Jim and take the life insurance proceeds."

"I was very desperate to have him (Jim) back," Gwen said. "I felt like I was at my limit and not really realizing that I actually was really having a breakdown."

With her husband not even dead yet, Gwen began purchasing clothes for herself and the children to wear for his funeral.

She bought silk flowers and boxes of Kleenex for mourning friends and family.

Gwen also increased the amount of Jim's life insurance from $300,000 to $1,000,000.

True to her premonition, she bought a wedding dress for herself and put a wedding ring on layaway for Knaack.

Gwen would ask God to speak to her directly and "guide her hand" as she thumbed through her Bible. When she got to a passage, she would believe that was what God wanted her to study."

"For the first reading, only the last sentence made sense," Gwen wrote. "I had asked if what I felt about Jim's death was real. He said yes.

God can even speak through the dictionary!

After reading the first page of stanzas, I knew I would be protected from car bombs, the knifings, the guns, the contracts and all the other evil I had seen connected with busting pornographers and pimps. Those Mafia guys play rough, but somehow they just won't be able to get me."

"You can see her delusions of grandeur in her journal writings," Smith said. "She had all of the symptoms of a delusional narcissist, truly believing that God made her as the 'Chosen One.'"

Gwen would write that she had a two-way conversation with God about creating the ranch.

"'Oh, so the ranch is in Douglas county near to the Springs so my family will be protected from the mafia guys' Then I knew in Denver, I'm Gwen Hendricks. In the Springs, I'm Gwen Knaack. I had thought the clinic would carry the name of the ranch, but with this new insight, I knew that for safety sake, everything had to be kept separate."

She continued to have health issues as well, as the nausea and attacks of dizziness still had not subsided. Physicians could not determine the cause of her illness. She was eventually diagnosed with Ménière's disease, an ailment that causes vertigo and a fluctuating hearing loss. She had a micro-shunt placed into her ear which only helped relieve the pain she was experiencing.

Her mental health, however, continued to deteriorate.

Jim would return to Colorado for good in May of 1991. It would not be a well-received reunion, however, as the couple fought over everything specifically the living arrangements of Knaack. Jim promptly kicked the boarder out of the home.

He then took control of the finances as he discovered that Gwen had maxed out the credit cards.

"My brother said that she had apparently taken several other credit cards and had maxed them out to the limit," recalled Steve Hendricks, Jim's brother. "And he was furious with her at that point. He did confide in me that he was thinking about leaving Gwen."

Jim would take away all of Gwen's credit cards and this made her extremely angry.

"He took away her power," Smith said. "She got an ego boost by buying expensive gifts for friends and helping out women that she thought were in need. When Jim took that away, she saw him as someone who needed to be eliminated."

Divorce seemed imminent but Gwen seemed immune to it all in her journal writings.

"The funeral, the ranch school, children, the foundation, always being pushed forward," she wrote. "I have to do what I have to do, too. But just for now I'm going to take one day at a time. I'm hoping I don't get too compulsed to do anything more for at least this coming week. I need to rest.

Perhaps I should start by explaining the little voice. It's my voice, but not me. It comes from somewhere inside, and if I don't listen to it, act on it, it becomes a compulsion. If I don't listen and act on the compulsion, it grows stronger and stronger until it dominates all aspects of my life. I learned long ago to listen and do what I'm told. Things work out when I do, and when I don't, things get real miserable...Yes, my little voice is the way God reaches me with the Holy Spirit."

With Jim now home on a permanent basis, The voices in her head grew louder. They began to speak with more urgency in telling her that she had to kill her husband.

"True to her religious background, she did not interpret auditory hallucinations as a sign of mental illness," Smith said. "Gwen was the kind of woman who took the stories in the Bible literally, seeing herself as a modern day Abraham who heard voices from God. You hear it in the way she describes the voices in her head telling her to sacrifice her husband in the same way the Bible speaks of God telling Abraham to sacrifice his son Isaac."

"I said 'Lord I surrender to you,'" Gwen recalled. "I'm hearing voices from God and this is what God wants and I have to get this from God and if this is what God wants then I have to give it to him. So I went out and I bought a gun"

"The voices in her head told her it was time," Smith said. "And true to her value system, she had to obey. For her religion was not a therapeutic aid because of the way she had viewed it. Her God was a vengeful one, a violent one."

On Friday, August 17th, 1991 Gwen drove to Peterson Air Force Base to meet with her husband, a 75 mile drive, to bring him a change of clothes.

"Jim was working late and he asked me to bring him something to eat." Gwen said.

She had informed police that Jim was working all night to prepare for an inspection but changed his mind.

Gwen wrote in her journal about the incident.

When Jim called to say he was on his way home, I went into shock. I knew the time was at hand. I knew I wasn't really ready. I screamed and cried and raged. Then I asked again, if he was meant to die or was I just suckered into some kind of head game. Benjamin's daddy died. I cried myself to sleep that night. I thought what was I supposed to do with two husbands. God has the oddest sense of humor."

"She told me that she was gonna make a nice little picnic for them," Gwen's step-daughter Season recalled. "They were going to make a night of it and that she wanted him to feel good for his inspection."

Gwen left the home and dropped off both Season and son Ben with a friend. When Gwen arrived at the Air Force base, however, she stated that Jim told her that he was heading home. She maintained that the two then went back home in separate cars.

"His truck was in the lead," Gwen said. "I was in the car behind. I remember being so tired, I told him I can't go on anymore. I just want a quick nap and let's get in the back of the truck."

She said that they traveled in separate cars but she became tired and slept through the night at a rest stop along Interstate 25.

Police, however, believed that Gwen lured Jim to an abandoned stretch of highway with the promise of sex.

The two met at the side of the road and Gwen hesitated when thinking of pulling out the gun. She wanted her husband to go peacefully.

"I took the gun out from underneath the seat of the car," Gwen said. "I got into the truck and laid next to him and when I could feel that he was deeply sleeping that's when I shot him."

Gwen would shoot Jim six times.

"It was like I was outside of myself," Gwen said. "Looking and watching what I was doing. I felt very numb, very cold, like I was on auto-pilot. I got back into my car and I took apart the gun and I was just throwing the parts out the window and just driving around, just in a fog, not knowing what I was doing, where I was going. I stopped at a roadside rest stop. Fell asleep. When I woke up and I didn't know everything that happened."

When Gwen arrived back home that Saturday she began making calls to the police, stating that her husband was missing.

On Monday morning, she called Jim's supervisor who sent out two officers to search for him.

One of his co-workers would find his pickup truck on the side of Highway 83 in Douglas County. His body had been placed in the camper shell in back of his truck.

He had been shot six times in the chest and neck with a small caliber handgun.

Gwen would become the primary suspect.

Police noted that she hardly showed any emotion when they informed her of her husband's death.

"Her state of mind was that of a wife with a missing husband," one of the deputies recalled. "When she was telling a story, she couldn't stick with the same story. And that's a clue, obviously, to law enforcement."

Gwen would then break the news to Jim's daughter, Season.

"Gwen said they found him by the side of the road in his car," Season said. "And that he had been murdered. I don't remember her crying. It was the worst moment of my life."

Terry Knaack would be helpful in the case against Gwen. She had been secretly in love with him and given him her diary. He read through her writings and promptly delivered the diary to the Douglas County Sheriff's Department. The sheriffs then instructed him to call Gwen while they would listen in.

Gwen would tell Knaack that she didn't kill Jim but that she wanted to die. Then Douglas County Sheriff's Department Kim Castellano's intuition told her something was wrong. The Hendricks had two pre-teens, a boy and a girl and the boy was never around during questioning.

Castellano believed that Gwen had a problem with males. With one of the male investigators, an Air Force official, by her side, Castellano went back to talk to Gwen.

Once again, the boy was not there. Gwen was overly polite to Castellano, asking her if she wanted anything to eat and jumping up to fix her something before she could answer.

Gwen would totally ignored the male detective.

Castellano used this knowledge to her advantage and befriended Gwen, sensing that the delusional woman would be much more forthcoming with a female officer than a male.

Gwen began trusting her enough that she asked for Castellano's help in balancing her check book. The detective then saw that

Hendricks had recently taken out several insurance policies that would be hers when her husband died.

The investigators then used a technique police refer to as the "midnight confession." Castellano and the Air Force official went over to the Hendricks house at eleven at night, waking Gwen up.

Questioning her in the family room, Gwen continued to deny her involvement in her husband's killing. Castellano and her partner then took turns reading from Gwen's journal, tightening the screws on her denial. They also saw Jim's watch on the counter.

Castellano then told her to get dressed and that she was being taken in.

Gwen finally cracked. She curled into a fetal position and confessed.

"Two stories that night—the story of the rest area and the story of Highway 83," she sobbed.

Gwen would go on to describe the highway story.

"There is blood everywhere, I can see it everywhere," she said. "It's terrible. My mind won't let me remember. I don't know if I shot him or not. I don't know what's real anymore."

Gwen was then taken to a local hospital where she stayed for two days for a mental health evaluation. She was arrested upon release and charged with her husband's murder.

After undergoing another mental health examination, Gwen was deemed delusional but understood the charges being levied against her.

Because of this, she was found fit to stand trial.

In court, however, Gwen continued to state that she didn't kill her husband. She said that the body found at the crime scene was not Jim's.

"There was the obvious choice for her attorneys to declare her insane," Smith said. "She had one hell of an imagination and could make things up on the fly. She said during the trial that she became completely convinced that her husband was still alive, going into full blown denial. 'He's still alive, he's out there somewhere and you have to find him', she would say. She was completely delusional."

Her first attorney, Lloyd Boyer, stated that it was physically impossible for Gwen to have murdered Jim Hendricks.

"The lack of gunshot residue inside the Capitol (Jim's car) vehicle," Boyer said. "Indicated that the murder had not occurred in the vehicle. Mr. Hendricks was quite a bit larger than Gwen and she was small, not especially strong and could not have moved the victim into the vehicle."

The investigators failed to produce the gun that Gwen used but the prosecution had another tool at its disposal.

The first link was Jim's watch that they found in Gwen's possession, which showed that she had tampered with the crime scene. The prosecution showed how she was going to use the money from the insurance policies and start a "home for troubled people" that would be near the spot where she killed her husband.

The jury found her guilty of first-degree murder and Hendricks was sentenced to life in prison.

"I just kept my faith that Jim would come rescue me and I would be set free from prison," Gwen said. "Of course, that never happened."

Inside the prison, physicians deemed her to be mentally unfit to be included with the general population and transferred her to the psychiatric unit.

"They got me on anti-psychotics," Gwen said. "And anti-depressants but it wasn't until 1997 that I started having memories of what had happened. At first, it was like just pictures and they hit me like bricks, you know. I killed a great husband and Dad. I robbed Season and Ben of their father. I felt lower than dirt."

She did have help, however, as some legal advocates filed briefs on her behalf, claiming that she had been insane at the time of her trial.

In September of 2000, the Supreme Court of Colorado overturned Gwen's conviction and ordered a new trial.

In April of 2001, a judge ruled that Gwen was not guilty by reason of insanity.

The trial lasted ten minutes.

"She came to terms with what she had done," Smith said. "She had stopped protesting, stop denying and admitted to what she had done."

Gwen was then remanded to a psychiatric care facility in Colorado. She then decided to change her name to "Emi Masai".

"When I lost Jim," Gwen said. "I also lost my children. I longed to be a wife and mother again. I redefined myself as married to Christ and being a mother to all the people I meet."

"By renaming herself she thought that she could obtain a new identity," Smith said. "It was a way of divorcing herself from her past transgressions."

Gwen went through four years of psychiatric treatment where the physicians determined that she was no longer a threat to society. She was released to a residential program where she now helps the needy at Mercy Ministries.

She continues to take her anti-psychotic medication.

"I never want to slip back into mental illness again," Gwen said. "I literally thank God every morning I open my medicine cabinet. I've always said justice wasn't done. Justice in this case would have been my execution. A life for a life. But it's not about fairness. It's about recognizing mental illness and knowing that you're not responsible for what you are doing when you're psychotic."

Gwen has had minimal contact with both her son and step-daughter since she committed the murder of their father.

"I long to see them but they let it be known through family channels that they don't want to see me," Gwen said. "So I respect that."

"I'm really glad that Gwen has helped herself enough to admit what she's done," Season said. "And I hope there never is a time where it gets easy for her to look in the mirror. Because there's never a time where it's easy to be without our Dad."

"I wish I could take it back," Gwen said. "Be a good wife and Mom again. I can't turn the clock back. So all I can do is give them my deepest apology and ask them to forgive me."

HOUSEWIFE, MOTHER & KILLER : THE TRUE STORY OF KIM HRICKO

DARLA PUGH

PROLOGUE

Kim Hricko was getting ready to kill her husband the night they attended a Valentine's Murder Mystery Party. Kim was a woman who was intelligent and determined, the irony of the play's theme was not lost on her.

It was destiny calling.

She watched with rapt attention as the actors went through the motions. A wedding bride took out a blue vial and poured the "poisonous" contents into her groom's champagne glass.

She has the right idea, Kim thought.

Looking over at her husband Steve, she imagined him in the place of the actor on stage, choking to death.

Could it be that easy?

CHAPTER ONE

"Kim Hricko was one of those people that you look at and say 'I would never have guessed,'" forensic psychologist Paula Orange said. "Something inside her snapped when she wanted out of her marriage. It could have been so simple. Call a lawyer and file for divorce. Kim wanted a lot more than that. She wanted blood."

Steve and Kim Hricko would be introduced by their mutual friends Maureen and Mike Miller at Penn State in 1984. Their temperaments seemed to be the perfect complement to one another, they would have a yin-yang compatibility.

"Kim was a very gregarious personality," Maureen said. "She was very outgoing. Very friendly. Everybody liked her."

"Steve was my best friend since seventh grade," Mike said. "Corny as it sounds we were kinda each others brother that we didn't have. My wife had set up a double date. He (Steve) was smitten by her. Thought she was very attractive. Basically, they hit it off and from that point on started dating."

Steve was a burly figure at 6'3" and 245 lbs. He was a star college football player but was on the shy side.

"He was a big teddy bear," Maureen said. "He just wanted everybody that he loved to be happy and for him to take care of them."

Neither Kim or Steve dated much before their union. Kim had a distant relationship with her father after her own parents divorced. Her mother would remarry a man that would sexually and physically abuse her.

Steve and Kim would marry and have a daughter. Nine years into their marriage, Steve would still be smitten by the woman that the Millers had set him up with. Kim, however, would have feelings of resentment that built up over time.

Temperamentally, the couple did not match up well. Steve was an introvert. Kim an extrovert. Kim hung out with doctors and nurses while Steve just wanted to stay home. He didn't feel welcome into Kim's elite social circle, put off by their large houses and flashy cars.

But Steve remained in love with Kim despite that over the years she did not treat him with the same warmth as she once did. She was now cold and disinterested toward her spouse.

Steve blamed himself for the deterioration and began working to save his marriage.

His efforts would only serve to pour fuel on the fire...

CHAPTER TWO

Kim fed up with the loveless relationship, suggested that they get a divorce but Steve refused. He also dismissed the idea of counseling but after nine years he finally saw it as a last resort.

Steve went to counseling on his own and began taking steps to show Kim how much he truly cared. One of the first things he did was write his wife a long, heartfelt love letter.

Kim shared the letter with some of her friends who remarked at how beautiful it was. But Steve's words of love and devotion had no effect on Kim.

"Can you believe this shit?" Kim mocked as she read some passages aloud. "I am willing to do whatever it takes to save our marriage. It takes two of us. But I know we can do it. Together."

"I think that's sweet," her friend remarked.

"Gag me," Kim rolled her eyes. "Trust me, when you've been married as long as I have this kind of syrupy shit only makes you sick."

"I wish my husband would write me love letters."

"No," Kim said. "You don't. They keep coming and they don't stop. He's smothering me and following me around the house like a puppy dog."

Steve's renewed efforts to rekindle a long dead marriage were now being met with resentment. He was earnest in displaying his affection and becoming more communicative with Kim.

"Let's talk about our feelings," he said to his wife who stiffened with his every touch.

Kim would go to work eager to vent. She would open up about her marital difficulties to anyone who was willing to listen. She found a confidante in Jennifer Gowen.

"He is suffocating me," Kim told Gowen. "Stifling me. Following me around the damn house the whole time and cuddling with me at night. I can't even breathe. He's always asking me where I'm going or what I'm doing. Now he's calling me on my cell just to say 'Hi'. He never used to do that. It is annoying as shit."

But Steve was merely following the advise of his counsel. He had not dated much before Kim and she was his first serious relationship. He had no idea what to do when the relationship turned sour.

"It has to be said that Steve was on the receiving end of some very bad counseling advice," Orange said. "Appeasement never works and that is something that any decent psychiatrist or counselor should know. He kept turning the other cheek with Kim and that just fueled her resentment of him even more. This isn't to justify his murder, of course."

With his counseling session inspired efforts not yielding any results, Steve became distraught. He had done everything by the book but it wasn't working. He called his close friend Mike and opened up about his marriage and job difficulties.

"I don't know what to do, man," Steve said, his voice quaking with emotion. "I don't want to lose her. She's my life. My family is my everything. I feel like I've already lost her."

"Take it easy," Mike said. "We'll figure something out."

"What do you think I should do?" Steve asked.

"You need to take her out," Mike said "Someplace special. You know. Make a memory."

"Yeah," Steve said. "I know that. But I'm at a loss at how to go about it. I've tried everything."

"Tell you what," Mike said. "You come over to the Golf Resort."

"Harbourtowne?"

"I'll make sure you get the honeymoon cottage we have here. The very best one."

"You're too cool, Mike."

"Anytime, brother."

Mike worked at the Harbourtowne Golf Resort and set up the accommodations for his good friend and his wife. The place was hosting a Valentine's Day Murder Mystery play. Mike knew that the place worked wonders for romance. If there was anyplace that could rekindle the spark in a relationship, the resort would be it.

But Steve didn't know that Kim already had a romance of her own. His name was Brad Winkler.

CHAPTER THREE

Kim had met Brad Winkler when she was planning out the bachelorette party for her co-worker, Jennifer Gowen. Jennifer had brought Brad to the wedding shower ahead of time and the United States Marine was the only man at the party aside from Steve.

Kim and the young man hit it off immediately. She gave him a ride home along with Norma Walz after the party was over. They dropped off Brad at his aunt's house and Kim watched from the car as the young man made his way inside.

"He was in a bad marriage," Kim said to Norma. "Pretty sad. He's a nice guy. Jesus. The girl who catches him is going to be a lucky one. He's really sweet."

Kim returned home and was chastised by Steve for spending so much time with Brad. He had no idea of the affair to come.

Jennifer Gowen would get married and enlist the aid of Brad to help around the house while she was away on her honeymoon. Jennifer had a one-year-old daughter and Brad would babysit the girl and do some chores around the place.

Kim would come over and help out with the baby on the day Gowen left.

The affair with Brad would begin that night. They would have their trysts at Jen's townhouse while his cousin was still on her honeymoon. When Jennifer returned, the couple would continue their affair at the home of Brad's aunt.

Kim was equally open about her affair with Brad Winkler among friends as she was about her dissatisfaction with her marriage.

"I'm seeing someone," Kim said to Rachel, her college friend.

"You're having an affair?"

"Its just sex," Kim said, shrugging her shoulder. "I'm not going to marry this guy."

Kim kept up the charade on the home front as she plotted her next move. The change in her behavior made Steve believe that his efforts were working as he chronicled in his journal.

"Life at home is improving," Steve wrote. "I am looking forward to Valentine's weekend at Harbourtowne with Kim. She called twice today and said 'I love you' without me saying it first. I was very happy. Kim and I have not made love yet and I want to but I will wait as long as it takes. I love her...I believe I know what being in love really is. We have been married nine years but I feel like we just started dating."

Sadly, four days after Steve wrote those words in his journal Kim was off buying Brad Winkler a Valentine's Day gift.

"Brad, I really want to give you all these gifts in person but I guess the Pentagon had a different idea," Kim wrote. "I am so proud of what you do so I'll just go on missing you. Have a nice weekend at home, baby. I look forward to seeing you soon. Happy Valentine's Day, sir. I love you so very much. Hugs and Kisses, Kim."

While Steve had an optimistic view of their future life together, Kim continued to tell anyone with a listening ear about her dissatisfaction.

"There is a lot of verbal abuse," Kim said to Theresa Armstrong, one of her neighbors. "From both of us. He doesn't do anything. I do everything. I am unhappy and don't want to be married to him anymore."

She then went to her job at Holy Cross Hospital and told her co-worker Norma Walz about her problems.

"I've been in a bad marriage for a long time," Kim said. "Me and Steve have been having problems for a long time. A very long time."

"I always suspected that something wasn't right," Norma said.

"I've been living a lie," Kim nodded. I wanted him to go to counseling two years ago. Now he's going. And he's driving me crazy."

Steve's constant fawning and pandering annoyed Kim so much that she began thinking about what life would be like without him.

"You know if my husband dies we'd be better off than if we got a divorce," Kim told one of her neighbors. "Steve doesn't make that much money. He's a groundskeeper. We get a divorce and I'm paying him alimony. But if he died, well, if he died we would inherit $450,000 from his life insurance."

"That's a morbid thing to think about," the neighbor said, trying to laugh it off.

"You read about these stories all the time. The husband killing off the wife and vice-versa. I always wondered why they did it instead of just getting a divorce. It's the life insurance. Just like in the movies."

"What was lost in Kim's rationalizing was the fact that the killers most always get caught," Orange said. "But in her mind, she was the special one. Narcissists always think like that. Like they are the special one that won't get caught. Still, Kim needed that reassurance from her peers that she was doing the right thing as crazy as it sounds."

After not getting a receptive response from her neighbor, Kim once again turned to Jennifer Gowen.

"Steve would be better off dead," Kim said, using the same line on Jennifer. "We talked about getting a divorce but Steve doesn't want that. Even if he did he is going to try and turn Anna against me or try to keep her. He doesn't have a life outside our marriage so he is better off dead anyway."

"You really shouldn't talk like that. Let alone think like that."

"Why not? I thought about telling him about Brad but I think he would just get depressed or suicidal. Then I would not be able to collect the insurance if he killed himself."

"You think he'd kill himself?"

"Probably," Kim said. "So I have to figure something else out. You know there was this serial killer. I forgot her name. But she would go around in the children's ward and shoot the kids up with Succinylcholine. It is a muscle paralyzer. No way to trace it."

Kim would later inform Gowen that if she could kill Steve and get away with it that she "would do it tomorrow."

Seeking other alternatives aside from poisoning, Kim approached fellow surgical tech Ken Burges in the locker room of the hospital.

"Hi, Ken."

"Hey there," Ken said.

"Do you know of anyone that could kill my husband?"

"What?" Ken asked. He thought Kim was playing a joke.

"Do you know anyone that can, you know, kill someone? For a price."

"I'm insulted that you would ask me that. Do I look that sketchy to you?"

Burges had been convicted of welfare fraud in Virginia a couple of years before obtaining his job at the hospital. Because of this, Kim may have presumed that he would be the type of person who would know people capable of such an act.

"I got $50,000 for anyone who could do something like that."

"You got the wrong dude," Ken said. "The wrong guy."

"Forget I even asked," Kim said.

"You work in the operating room," Ken advised. "You could just put him to sleep."

Ken didn't know that Kim already had that idea in mind.

Kim began to plot out details of the murder. She needed to do something that was untraceable. This called for poison. She had to burn away any evidence so her attack had to take place away from home.

She ran her plan by a college friend of hers, Rachel McCoy. Kim justified her actions by demonizing her husband. She talked about his unwillingness to do stuff with her as he was a homebody and kept a messy home. Their personalities were too different.

Then without warning, she began articulating her plan to kill Steve with the poison and then setting the place on fire.

It was almost as if she wanted Rachel to poke any holes in her plan should she miss anything.

Rachel tried to talk Kim out of the hare-brained idea to no avail. She suggested simply getting a divorce but Kim was convinced that killing Steve was "easier." Rachel also brought up the fact that she was robbing their daughter, Anna, of a father.

"She would be better off without him," Kim said.

Whatever Rachel suggested, Kim had an answer for.

Her mind was made up.

Steve had to go.

CHAPTER FOUR

Kim knew that the drug she had to obtain was Succinylcholine. It would be readily available to her as she did her rounds through the hospital. Just walk by a tray of meds in the surgery unit and lift one of the vials. Easy peasy.

"I'm going to get this drug," Kim told her friend Rachel. "It will paralyze Steve. Stop his breathing and then I'll set the curtains on fire with a candle or a cigar. He won't be able to move and then he'll die of smoke inhalation. Nobody will know shit."

Kim would not take into account the fact that her husband was a healthy and robust man with no medical history. That would certainly draw suspicion.

"This would be the only logical explanation for what brought about Steven Hricko's death," prosecuting attorney Robert Dean said.

"Because there was nothing else wrong with him. His body organs were in fine shape, there was no trauma. It had to have been this. She had to have carried through her plan."

"Kim was determined," Orange said. "She wanted her cake and eat it too. It is a head scratcher as to why she didn't pursue a divorce but the mind of a sociopath works differently. She wanted a clean break. If she had gotten a divorce, then Steve would have remained in her life forever the next ten years because of their daughter. She wanted to erase him from the picture and nothing and nobody was going to talk her out of it."

The planned romantic getaway loomed on the horizon for Valentine's Day weekend. Steve looked forward to their alone time together with giddy excitement. He told his counselor that this would be the turning point where the sparks of romance would once again be rekindled.

But Kim looked toward the weekend with dread. She had told Jennifer Gowen that she had only had sex with Steve once in the past six months and the experience left her feeling repulsed.

"I'm not looking forward to the trip," Kim said in her own counseling session.

"Why?" her counselor asked. "It may be an opportunity to rekindle some passion."

"I'm tired and really don't feel up to the trip. It's a long drive. It is going to be miserable."

Then a light bulb flashed in Kim's mind. The resort would be the perfect place.

The perfect place to put her plans into effect.

CHAPTER SIX

Valentine's Day weekend arrived.

Steve had romance on his mind. His forehead perspired as he felt the anxiety of trying to save his marriage.

Kim had Brad Winkler on her mind as she looked out the car window.

Then her mind drifted to murder.

She had to set everything up just right. Inject Steve. Burn the cottage room. Then tell the police her story and stick with it no matter what.

Kim and Steve drove from their home in Laurel, Maryland to St Michaels. It would be a 75-mile to a romantic getaway that many had christened as the "Heart & Soul of Chesapeake Bay."

But the couple arrived at their cottage and found the place to be freezing. Kim started a fire in the wood stove then made some coffee.

The conversation was muted and awkward. They decided to watch some TV before looking out the window and taking in the view of the bay. It was windy and the the cold, damp weather chased them back inside

Preparing for the dinner, Steve popped a few Effexor tablets for his depression which had gotten worse in recent weeks. He also took an anti-anxiety medication called Xanax and a muscle relaxant called Flexeril.

Getting dressed, they attended the interactive murder mystery dinner called THE BRIDE WHO CRIED. The actors staged a re-enactment of a woman killing her soon to be husband. The actors encouraged audience members to ask the actors questions in an attempt to find out who the murderer was.

Kim enjoyed the play immensely. When the actors called for audience participation, she was one of two women who went out onto the stage and began asking questions like a detective.

The play now over, Kim and Steve returned to their cottage. Not yet having their fill of entertainment, the couple would watch the comedy film "Tommy Boy". They got a good laugh out of it but according to Kim they "still did not talk about our problems."

Steve then fell asleep.

Kim stood over him like a predator then went to the bathroom to prepare her lethal cocktail of succinylcholine. Building up her nerve, she finally did the move that she had been practicing in her head for two years.

Kim pulled aside the bed sheet and injected the syringe into his neck.

I'll burn the body. That will get rid of the puncture wound.

Kim also knew that the drug she administered only caused paralysis. It didn't affect a patient's level of consciousness.

So when Kim set the room on fire, Steve would know that he was being burned to death.

And he wouldn't be able to do anything about it.

The thought made Kim smile. She didn't want to just kill him. She wanted to make him suffer. To humiliate him.

Kim pulled the now paralyzed but awake Steve off the bed and dropped him to the floor. She doused his body with lighter fluid.

Kim, what are you doing? Steve looked up at his wife, unable to move or speak.

"Call it the perfect crime," she whispered in his ear as if reading his thoughts.

He stared straight up at the ceiling, catching Kim's movements in the corner of his eye.

He heard a matchstick strike against a box.

Then he felt a sharp pain race up his body as she set him ablaze.

I can't move, Steven thought as terror and pain engulfed him.

I can't breathe.

I can't breathe.

Kim, what are you doing?

I brought you here to save our marriage. I have done what I could do making this better.

I love you. Please don't do this!

Kim poured more of the lighter fluid onto Steve's body. She lit another match and threw it on him.

"She injected him with succinylcholine and watched him suffocate," Maureen said. "And lit him on fire. How much colder could it get."

CHAPTER FIVE

Kim Hricko walked into the resort reception area with a calm demeanor. She had her ear to her cell phone which was turned upside down.

"I need to talk to someone who works here," she informed desk clerk Elaine Phillips.

"I work here," Elaine said, expecting Kim's response being anything from wanting more towels to complaining about faulty air conditioning.

"My room is on fire."

"Is there anyone else in the room?" Phillips asked.

"Yeah," she said without emotion. "My husband."

"What room are you in?" Elaine asked, making her way around the corner of the desk.

Elaine and another hotel employee hurried into the courtyard of the resort.

"You smell that?" Elaine asked. "Something is definitely burning."

The two sprinted to cottage number 506 at the end of the resort. The door was shut but there was a tiny opening in the sliding door in the rear.

Smoke filled the room. They could barely see one foot in front of them. Kneeling down, one of the employees saw the the prone figure of a man inside. He crawled in, braving the smoke and pulled the body to safety on the back porch.

It was too late.

Steve Hricko, burned to a crisp.

The man had died with a Playboy magazine at his side with his pajama pants down at his knees as if he collapsed while masturbating.

"I want to see his dead body," Kim said as she milled around with the hotel guests watching the scene.

"I thought it was odd," one of the guests said. "Because no one had pronounced anyone to be dead yet."

Kim gave her statement to the Sheriff then called their best friends, Mike and Maureen Miller.

"It's the last thing you expect when you receive a phone call at night," Maureen said. "When the phone rings at night you know that it's not anything good."

"My wife answered the phone," Mike Miller said. "And sort of roused me a little bit and said that there's was an incident in Steve and Kim's room. Kim's requesting that you come down there as soon as possible.

The Millers were shocked at the sudden death of Steve. They were even more shocked at the demeanor of Kim when they went to console her.

"I didn't expect her to be anything less than a hysterical woman whose husband passed away," Maureen said. "She was the exact opposite. Just exact opposite."

Kim told everyone that Steve was drunk and made advances toward her. He groped and fondled her but she didn't want to have sex. They argued and she left the cottage.

Mike knew that something was fishy. His friend Steve was not a drinker.

Did Kim plan this out?

"They said the fire started because of him carelessly smoking," Mike said. "Steve doesn't smoke. All the years I've known Steve, I've never seen him smoke a cigarette, a cigar. He despised being around people that smoked."

An autopsy was performed and forensic pathologist Janis Amatuzio, like Mike Miller, quickly realized that something was amiss.

"Steven's body was found in a fire," Amatuzio said. "The major question for the forensic pathologist is that did he die of the fire or not. When there was no soot in the airways, when there was no damage to the lungs. It suggested that Steven was dead before the fire started."

"Steven was not drunk that night," prosecuting attorney Robert Dean said. "The drug tests and the autopsy shows that. Steve was not drunk."

The picture didn't fit. Steve was not a drinker nor was he a smoker. But friends and family could not believe the worst about Kim Hricko. The fun and outgoing mother could not have killed her own husband, the man who adored her for the past nine years.

Could she?

"Was she really capable of doing this?" Maureen asked. "Everybody was saying it but again, I ignored it and just pushed it back and said that she wasn't capable of doing it. Man, was I wrong."

CHAPTER SIX

Police began their investigation and discovered that Kim left a trail of incriminating conversations as well as evidence.

"Kim was too smart for her own good," Orange said. "She did her research on succinylcholine, did her research on the how quickly a body burns. But she did not know how to stage a killing."

Kim had left empty beer bottles in the room and a pack of cigars. The cigars would be the clue that blew Kim's story up in smoke.

Steve was not a smoker and the cigars she had left behind as evidence were not the kind to start a fire.

"There was an investigation as to how a fire like this could have started," prosecuting attorney Robert Dean said. "That fire could not have started by the ashes of a cigar."

Kim would state that after she and Steve had gotten into a fight she went for a drive. She wanted to visit Mike and Maureen Miller who only lived minutes away. She stated she had become lost. The prosecution thought that her excuse seemed odd as she had visited the Millers on numerous occasions. She also had a brother who lived only a few blocks away from the Miller home. And why had she not simply called them on her cell phone?

"I didn't want to wake anyone," Kim said when asked why she didn't call.

Her answer was incongruent as why would she worry about waking someone up with a cell phone call when she didn't have a problem arriving on their doorstep in the middle of the night?

Nine days after the murder, police would arrive at the home of a Hricko friend where Kim had been staying. They had a search warrant for her car but Kim felt the noose tightening around her neck. She ran to the bathroom room and locked it behind herself as the police entered the home.

Kim then swallowed a whole bottle of Xanax.

"Come out of there, Kim," the police yelled.

They busted the door down and saw Kim there in the bathtub, holding a razor blade over her wrist.

"I'll kill myself!" she screamed. "I'll fucking do it!"

The officers quickly subdued Kim without further incident. They then transported her to a psychiatric facility where she was put on suicide watch.

The trial would only last six days as the prosecuting attorney detailed how Kim staged the murder.

"She stated that he was sloppy drunk," prosecuting attorney Robert Dean said. "And that he wanted to have sex. She said they got into an argument and that she left for a few hours. She said she drove around and got lost. And then she returned to the cottage and saw that it was full of smoke and then she reported that the room was on fire."

The case against Kim was made by several friends, co-workers, and neighbors. They all testified about the affair, the plot to kill Steve and her desire to acquire the drug succinylcholine.

Kim Hricko would be found guilty of murder and arson. She would be sentenced to life in prison.

"It's sad that he (Steve) is not the one in the world anymore and she is," Maureen said.

"He was my best friend," Mike said. "And the fact that he isn't here anymore is pretty hard for me to take."

The other victim aside from Steve was their nine-year-old daughter. She lost both her father and her mother.

"Her child is the victim," Maureen said. "And is forever going to wonder which side of the family is telling the truth. Is it true that her mother was unjustly accused or is it true that she's a cold, manipulating, calculating murderer."

END

DANA SUE GRAY

KAREN COLLIER

Dana Sue Gray was born on December 6th, 1957 in Pasadena, California. Her mother, Beverly Arnett, was a former beauty queen who worked as a professional model. Her father, Russell Armbrust, worked as a hairdresser and was married three times prior to marrying Beverly. The couple had several miscarriages before Dana was born.

Her mother was born for the camera and loved attention. She liked being pampered, getting her make-up done and wearing flashy outfits. Beverly modeled for Bullock's, did print ads for Hamilton watches and was once a Rose Princess at the Tournament of Roses Parade.

LIKE MOTHER LIKE DAUGHTER

Russell divorced Beverly, however, when he witnessed his wife attack an older woman that had angered her. Beverly had also maxed out his credit cards, putting him financial peril. Dana was only two years old at the time of the divorce and rarely saw her father.

"Some kind of estrangement had taken place," forensic psychologist Lora Dixon said. "After her parents divorced she had turned down invitations in her teen years to visit her father on all of the holidays and birthday get-togethers."

"There is also something to think about here in terms of Beverly's own temper. Dana clearly witnessed violence and bullying from her mother at an early age. She inherited those characteristics from her mother with tragic results."

Dana had discipline problems early on as she sought attention from her narcissistic mother. Her mother would discipline her but Dana would retaliate by stealing money to buy candy. Her mother had two other children from a previous marriage. Dana would go into the rooms of her step brothers and urinate in their beds.

Her mother would continue to try and discipline her to no avail as Dana would lash back with violence. This facet of her personality was never placed under her control.

"Mommy and daughter didn't get along," Dixon said. "But obviously that isn't unusual nor does mean she was destined to become a serial killer. There was some deep seated issues festering here though. This is evident when Dana gave her mother a snake for Christmas. 'A snake for a snake' the card must have read."

Nonetheless, it did not appear on the surface that Dana had to endure the brutal childhood that gave birth to so many other serial killers. Cedric Ward, one of her step brothers, did admit that Dana did not have the best of childhoods. "It was not happy growing up," he recalled.

SCHOOL AND SEX

Dana did not get along with other students and achieved low grades in all of her classes. She was a chronic truancy case and often forged notes to get out of class. Dara was sexually active at a very early age as she would lose her virginity at the age of twelve. She would ultimately go from one relationship to the next, using sex to lure men into her web of narcissism.

"Dana has a problem," said Richard Singer, a boyfriend of her mother. "She does not want to be told no. She has her own thing, and nobody could tell her any different. You could not tell Dana what to do."

"Her mother would pretty much try to control her, but Dana would go off on you. You could not tell her what to do. Dana is very hyperactive and opinionated."

During her adolescent years, she loved horror movies and read Grimm's Fairy Tales numerous times. As a teenager, she and a neighbor built a catapult. They would tie tiny parachutes on the cat's backs and then hurl them into the air, with the parachute carrying them down into neighborhood swimming pools.

A MOTHER'S DEATH

Beverly contracted breast cancer when Dana was fourteen. Dana decided to become a nurse after witnessing the way the nurses at the hospital treated her mother. Her mother died and Dana was forced back to live with her father.

"The temptation here is to say that Dana was inspired to become a nurse by witnessing the compassion the nurses shown her mother during her illness," Dixon said. "But I would posit a different psychological scenario. Dana saw that the nurses had power over her mother. That for once, her mother was weak and had to defer to other people for the first time in her life. Dana wanted power. Control. What better way to get that then to become a nurse?"

Dana went into a depression after her mother died and would reveal her sentimentality in letters she would write to her then boyfriend, Don Lane, in jail.

"Tomorrow, Good Friday, 4-1-94, is also April Fool's and also my real mom's 76th B-day. It's been 22 years since her death, and I still celebrate her B-day for her. I celebrate it for her 'cause she died when I was 14 and we never got to get past the 'grow years' to become friends like my dad and I are. She was wild-but made my younger years a total adventure: camping, clamming @ Pismo, best Halloween parties and the best Xmases a poor family could have. She could make a fun time out of just anything."

"Again, you see in her letters a sense of victimhood," Dixon said. "She makes no mention of her mother ignoring her birthdays. And she describes her family as 'poor.' They lived in relatively affluent area, becoming strapped for cash primarily because of Beverly's spending."

GROWING UP

Dana's father Russell had remarried, living with his new wife Yvonne who had a daughter named Cathy. Dana would move in with the couple, sharing a room with Cathy. The reunion between her and her father would be a short-lived one, however, as Yvonne would find marijuana in Dana's room.

Russell's wife then kicked Dana out of the home.

On her own at the age of fifteen, Dana would move-in with her sky-diving instructor, Rob Beaudry. The union would produce two pregnancies but Rob talked Dana in to getting abortions both times. These were decisions that she would later come to resent.

At five-foot-two and weighing a stocky 135 lbs, Dana would nonetheless inherit her mother's penchant for fancy clothes and desire to be pampered with manicures and pedicures. Despite her taste in high-end living, associates would describe her appearance and demeanor as "hard."

She would graduate from Newport High School in 1976 and enter nursing school at Saddleback College in Mission Viejo, California. Dana paid her way through nursing school while working as waitress. She also taught herself screen printing techniques and sold screen printed items for extra cash.

"Dana inherited her mother's psychology when it came to money and relationships," Dixon said. "She operated from a 'lack mindset', in that she always saw herself as poor. She was industrious but felt sorry for herself that she had to work so hard, paying her way through school and working for a living. The shopping sprees were a relief to her perceived burden."

ESTRANGED FROM FAMILY

Dana became estranged from her half-brothers, her older siblings from Beverly's previous marriage. The reasons were always financial as she become embroiled in a dispute over the proceedings from their aunt's estate.

She had run-ins with her half-brother Rick in particular.

Dana reacted with anger after he told her to sell belongings to pay her mounting bills. Rick wrote back telling her that she had no consideration for others.

"Nuts," is how her sister-in-law described her. "Not even normally greedy. Crazy. Gray is missing a conscience. I do not think it is there. When you talk to her, she has no concept of other human beings."

"The half-brothers clearly knew she was trouble," Dixon said. "They did the right thing in distancing themselves.

NURSING CAREER.

Immediately upon graduating from Saddleback, Dana landed a nursing job at Corona Community Hospital. She used that as a springboard to a high paying position as an operating room nurse at Inland Valley Regional Medical Center (some reports have her identified as a labor and delivery nurse). She was described by one nursing supervisor as "very caring."

During this time, she had found another boyfriend, a windsurfer whom she would accompany on trips to Hawaii where they would pursue various outdoor activities. This relationship would be an on-again, off-again type deal until Dana would marry Tom Gray. The couple would tie the knot at a winery in the affluent Temecula area.

Tom was an active sportsman and had a crush on Dana since high school.

"She was a hard core athlete," Tom recalled. "A sky diver, wind surfer, mountain bike enthusiast and snorkeler, and she was skilled in each sport."

Dana took pride in her physical strength and would often roll up her sleeve to reveal her bicep muscle. 'She how strong I am?' she would ask.

Living in the gated community of the affluent Canyon Lake suited Dana as it would have been something that would have pleased her mother. Her and Tom started numerous businesses where they used the name "Graymatter."

Tom could not stop Dana's spending habits, however. The couple took out a loan for $47,000 and another for $20,000 within the first nine months of their marriage.

"She was replicating the marriage of her mother and father," Dixon said. "She liked the empowerment that came from having a lot of money. Having money, or rather the act of spending money is what fed her ego. Only in Dana's case she took it way beyond her mother. She was willing to kill for that feeling."

The marriage quickly soured when Dana's spending habits sent the couple into overwhelming consumer debt. Her alcoholism also worsened, particularly after she suffered a miscarriage. Dana indulged in three or four glasses of wine while cooking dinner and then having more with the dinner itself. Her days off from the hospital were adventures in bourbon whiskey, 7-Up and Tequila shooters. Later, she would admit to using marijuana and cocaine.

When Gray unexpectedly received a $7500 inheritance, Dana took the money and blew it on a trip to Europe, leaving her husband behind at home. When she returned , she began an affair with Don Lane, a musician in her husband's band. When Lane agreed to support her, she moved out of the Canyon Lake house and spent $11,000 in five months.

In March of 1992, however, Dana began seeing a psychiatrist. He prescribed Paxil for her, probably to stave off depression among other things.

Lane had a five year old son at the time and would later tell authorities of Dana's "mood changes" and her propensity to break out into "hysterical tears" with little provocation.

She filed for divorce from Tom but this would not be finalized until much later. In September of 1993, Tom and Dana were forced to file for bankruptcy to prevent foreclosure on their Canyon Lake residence.

Despite the value of the home increasing, the amount they owed on the house was more than its worth. They owed $177,500 on a house valued at $125,000 because of double mortgages.

She suffered a miscarriage, exacerbating more depression as well as alcohol and drug abuse.

FIRED FROM THE HOSPITAL

The trouble continued for Dana as two months later she would be fired from the hospital for stealing Demerol and other opiate pain killers.

"What Dana was trying to do was medicate herself," Dixon said. "The new marriage, the exotic vacations, the fancy house and cars. It was never enough to quell the demons that spoke in her head. A control freak out of control. So she struggled to constantly fill the void with booze and drugs. Then this spirals into an affair with a friend of her husband. Again, this life trajectory happens to a lot of people. In Dana's case, however, she needed that extra thrill. Something more than the rush of sky-diving, cheating on her husband, and getting high. She needed the ultimate adrenaline rush. The power to take someone's life."

TIME TO KILL

In later reports, hospital authorities would reveal their own problems with Gray.

"She is sarcastic," Darlena Addison, the former nursing supervisor who fired Gray for stealing drugs. "She does get her point across if she's crossed or doesn't get her way."

"The problem was a condescending attitude, as Dana believed that she was smarter than everyone and had a need to dominate."

The hospital would later report that they did not have any "unusual" deaths during Gray's tenure.

"Of course that is what you would expect them to say," Dixon said. "If they admit to any 'unusual' deaths then it certainly opens them up to a lawsuit. The opportunity would certainly be there for Dana to steal credit cards from elderly patients and rack up bills. It appears, however, that she did not put her murderous impulses into action until after her dismissal. Dana fell in love with the struggle. The fight of her victim as long as she would emerge on he winning end. Poisoning her victims to death in the way it would have been possible for her as a nurse would not have given her that adrenaline rush."

After the loss of her job, Dana would amp up her indulgences in alcohol, drinking straight Vodka, loving the Smirnoff brand in particular.

On Valentine's Day in 1994, Dana contacted Tom's parents (after their separation he had kept his phone number and address a secret). She informed Tom's parents that she wanted to meet with him.

Tom agreed at first but later did not show up.

Tom would find out that Dana had taken out an insurance policy on him without his knowledge. The policy payout would have been enough to pay down the Canyon Lake home the couple used to share.

Later that day, Dana murdered Norma Davis.

THE FIRST VICTIM

Norma Davis was 86 years old at the time. She was the mother-in-law of the woman (Jeri Davis Armbrust) who married Dana's father in 1988. Jeri's first husband, Bill Davis, was Norma's son. Bill died in the early 1980s, and his widow married a newly divorced Russell.

But Jeri continued to care for her elderly mother-in-law, even after she remarried. Dana would also come to know Norma very well.

On February 16th, 1994, however, the body of Norma Davis would be found by a neighbor named Alice Williams. She had been dead for two days as someone had stabbed her in the neck with a wood-handled utility knife. The blade had been inserted so deep that it nearly severed Norma's head.

She also had a filet knife sticking out of her chest.

Police would discover no forced entry into the home. Norma always kept the doors locked unless she was expecting a visitor. Her neighbor, Alice, stated that she could not remember if Norma had mentioned she was expecting company.

"We didn't have a lot of information," Detective Joe Greco said. "The only piece of evidence that we had was the entry way of the condominium. There was a faint shoe print on the condominium and it was a 6 ½ size shoe."

Detectives would find the Nike shoe print and Davis' Social Security check in plain view. Additionally, on the first floor of the condo, they found a smear of blood on an armchair and a torn phone cord.

A modus operandi had been established. Dana would manually strangle her victims with a phone cord, then use an object to smash or stab.

The coroner concluded that Norma Davis was strangled first then stabbed. She was stabbed eleven times with Dana leaving the knives stuck in her body.

Police described the scene as one of the most brutal they had ever encountered.

"It was a shock because it was only my second homicide case as a detective," Greco said. "It was overwhelming. It crossed my mind that I had a serial killer on my hands."

SHE DEVIL ON A RAMPAGE

"The community was very affluent," Greco said. "They don't have a lot of homicides."

On February 28th, 1994, 66-year old June Roberts was found murdered. She had lived in the gated community of Canyon Lake along with Dana.

Dana had known Roberts and visited her that day saying that she wanted to borrow a book about either overcoming alcohol addiction or vitamins, the reports vary. Dana had her boyfriend's five year old son waiting out in front in her Cadillac.

Ignorant of Dana's true motives, Roberts allowed Dana into her home. She went to retrieve the book Dana inquired about while her would-be killer ripped out the cords to June's phone

Dana would later describe their interaction taking a turn when she became "really annoyed" that June came back with the wrong book. She also told a psychologist that she became infuriated that June allegedly said that she "didn't do enough" to save her marriage with Tom.

When asked what made Dana believe that Roberts and her other victims were looking down on her, Dana responded that she did not like their body language.

"The arching of the eyebrow," Dana said. "That is what happened. All three."

Dana then used the phone cord to strangle Roberts to death.

"I was right behind her," Dana recalled. "I choked her with the phone cord. She was holding on, trying to get the cord off. I pulled her down. She was on her back. I hit her in the head with a bottle. I lost it. I was so consumed. I don't know the time span in there-must have been very quick. She must have stopped moving, and I left. As I walked out, she had a little wallet thing. I grabbed it."

"We went out and proceeded to shop up a storm. "

In talking to psychologists,.Dana appeared unaware of the concept of remorse.

"It was very brutal," Greco said. "The victim had been strangled with her own telephone cord and actually tied to a chair. And she was struck so hard (by the wine bottle) she fractured her skull."

Her autopsy noted a "moderately deep ligature furrow" and a "6 x 3 purple contusion." The cranium contusion was caused by a heavy glass wine bottle striking her with tremendous force. The volume of blood in and near the bathroom door, the walls and pooling under the body made it impossible to gauge the age of the victim.

"This is when the profile of Dana Sue becomes highly unusual," Dixon said. "With female serial killers, you usually see poison or the use of a gun as the weapon of choice. Dana Sue, however, approached her victims with a high level of physical violence that rivaled a male serial killer. There was nothing lady-like about her approach. She was a cold blooded, hands on killer."

TIME TO SHOP

Dana did not hesitate after murdering Roberts, she had to get her shopping fix met.

She would go to Bally's Wine Country Cafe in Temecula, eat crab cake and scampi while charging the meal to Robert's credit card. She could not finish the entire meal, however, and had the waitress pack the rest.

She then got an eyebrow wax and a perm then treated her boyfriend's son to a stylish haircut.

"The fact that she had the little boy accompany her on both the murders and the shopping trips deserves mention," Dixon said. "Dana remained childless throughout life. She was regretted getting two abortions and suffered a miscarriage during her marriage with Tom. Going out and about with her boyfriend's son made her feel like a Mommy. She could be the Mommy that she never had, treating the young child to things she always wanted."

Dana signed "June Roberts" on the $164.76 charge at the salon. She then went to the mall and spent $511 on a black suede jacket, several pairs of cowboy boots, and then $161 on a pair of diamond earrings all charged to Roberts. Her addiction still not satiated, she went to a drug store, picking up dog treats, two bottles of Smirnoff and a toy police helicopter for the boy.

The day after, Dana loaded up on suntan lotion, got a massage at Murrieta Hot Springs resort and then went on another power shopping spree.

"She had absolutely no remorse," Dixon said. "There was no hiding out and laying low like some other wimpy male serial killer. Dana Sue was different. She killed and then she had to do the one thing that gratified her. She had to get to the mall. She had to get the high from buying stuff. She had to enjoy the power while it still lasted."

Ironically, none of her victims had anything stolen aside from their credit cards.

"Dana didn't take any rings from her victims," Greco said. "Or some valuables from the home that were obvious. So I don't think any of the crimes were motivated by money."

Ten days after the Roberts' murder, Dana would enter an antique store, the Main Street Trading Post in Lake Elsinore. Dana stated to the cashier, Dorinda Hawkins, that she wanted to buy a picture frame for a photo of her deceased mother.

"Dana came in asking about picture frames," Greco said. "During their interaction, Dana felt that Dorinda was being condescending to her.

"I felt sick to my stomach," Dana said. "I wanted to vomit. I wanted her to die."

Dana asked if Hawkins was working alone and then she attacked her, strangling her with the store's telephone cord.

"Dorinda is begging for her life when Dana is strangling her," Greco said. "And Dorinda told her 'you can have anything you want. Take the cash, I have eight kids, just let me live.' And Dana told her 'I'm not doing this for the money.' She said that twice. And that really gives you an insight on what Dana is thinking while she's committing these crimes."

Dorinda, however, continued to fight, resisting Dana all the way.

"Relax," Dana said, trying to coax Hawkins into dying. "Just relax."

Hawkins grabbed a broom and poked Dana with it to no avail.

Dana then shoved Hawkins to the ground and stepped on her head as a brace to better choke her.

"Her eyes were flat," Hawkins recalled. "I could tell she had killed before."

Believing her victim dead, Dana stole five dollars from Hawkins' purse and twenty dollars from the cash register.

An hour later, she began another shopping spree, still using Roberts' credit cards.

Hawkins, however, would survive the attack and provide the police the required description of Dana.

THE ATTACKS CONTINUE

Nearly a month after her first killing, on March 16th, 1994, Dana would kill the 87-year old Dora Beebe.

Moments after Beebe arrived home from a doctor's appointment, Dana pulled up in front of her house. She knocked on the door and asked Beebe for directions.

"Here we see Dana getting bolder," Dixon said. "With Norma Davis and June Roberts, she knew the victims beforehand. And the attempted murder in the antique store seemed to be a spur of the moment thing. But the Beebe murder is the first occasion where Dana has picked out a stranger. Elderly women were her preferred target, specifically those who were alone, and tragically Beebe emerged in her cross-hairs."

Living in the same neighborhood for several years, it was improbable for Dana to become lost. But she used that as an excuse when she came knocking on Beebe's door asking for directions.

Dana became angry when Beebe said "I don't have time for this." She was able to hide her anger as Beebe capitulated and allowed Dana insider her home to look at a map. Once inside the home, however, Dana assaulted the elderly woman.

'She turned her back on me," Dana said. "I choked her with the phone cord. I hit her in the head with an iron. As I remember it, it wasn't much of a fight."

Using a stainless steel Black and Decker iron that Dana found in the home, Dana bashed Beebe in the head so hard that it dented the appliance.

Less then an hour later, Dana would be at the mall with Beebe's credit cards in hand.

"She enjoyed doing things that were risky," Greco said. "She was a thrill seeker. I think that she really enjoyed what she was doing. She got a thrill out of it."

PANIC IN THE STREETS

The residents in the gated community of Canyon Lake went into panic mode. Some of the elderly citizens moved in with family until the killer was caught. A group of elderly widows organized themselves to sleep together at designated houses, not wanting to be alone.

There were some who thought the killings where the product of a cult engaging in the ritual sacrifice of the elderly.

"Rumors circulated around the entire community," Dixon said. "A terrifying time for everyone, the elderly in particular. This was a relatively well-to-do neighborhood. People were unused to killings, let alone a serial killer. Numerous people bought guns and kept it by their bedside while others banded together in the belief that there were safety in numbers."

FALSE SUSPECT

Police detectives were at a loss early on in finding a suspect. Prospects were so bleak that a supervisor in charge had seriously thought about using a psychic. Dana was not anywhere near the police's list of possible killers. Instead, the police initially suspected that her mother-in-law, Jeri Armbrust, might be the killer.

The police determined that Armbrust used to be married to Davis' son and continued to care for her former mother-in-law.

Detectives grew suspicious because it was unusual that Jeri would continue to take care of someone who was not a blood relative. Norma Davis herself was on death's door, recovering from a triple bypass surgery.

Police determined that Jeri had been in Davis' house the Sunday before the murder and that she wore a pair of Nike shoes.

Jeri stated that she did come to Davis' house but only came to drop off groceries. She heard the TV on upstairs but did not go up to say hello. She left the groceries on the counter and went home.

Police questioned why she didn't say hello but after weeks of questioning police determined that Jeri was not a suspect. She instead became an ally to the investigation.

CAPTURE

Descriptions obtained from the various merchants at the shopping center were eventually used to catch Dana. She had been buying so much stuff that the credit card company called June Roberts' family to inquire about the excessive spending.

Police detectives went to all of the stores where Roberts' credit card had been used, interviewing the cashiers. They obtained a physical description of Dana, surmising that the killer had dyed her hair recently and was accompanied by a little boy.

Detective Greco relayed this information to Jeri Armbrust.

Jeri surmised that the killer was in fact, her step-daughter Dana. She said that Dana recently dyed her hair red and had a boyfriend who had a young son.

Greco then obtained a search warrant and called for the aid of ARCNET (Allied Riverside County Narcotics Enforcement Team) to stake out Gray's home in Lake Elsinore.

Unfortunately, Dana was murdering Dora Beebe just hours before they determined her to be the killer. They followed Dana to a bank where she used Beebe's credit card and then went out for another shopping spree.

"We were able to follow the paper trail created by the use of these credit cards," Greco said. "With the merchants we were able to get a general description of the suspect."

Later that day, Greco arrested Dana while she was cooking dinner. Assisting officers took her boyfriend and his son in for questioning.

HOUSE OF STOLEN GOODS

Police did a thorough search of Dana's home after her arrest.

"They found jewelry, food, liquor, a ski mask, a purse with nearly $2,000 stuck in the washing machine, and many items of clothing," one report stated. "The police obtained a wealth of evidence: Gray's use of credit cards, clerks who had seen her directly after each murder, handwriting experts who identified her signatures on various items."

Dana was interrogated for hours.

"In the interview," Greco recalled. "Dana talked about finding a purse. And that purse belonged to a woman by the name of Dora Beebe. I knew that I had the right suspect in this case. But I didn't not know that on the same day we were serving her search warrant she was killing her last victim."

Dana stated that she never took the credit cards but after police revealed that they had evidence of her using them, Dana claimed that she found both Roberts' and Beebe's cards.

She maintained this story throughout the questioning. When asked why she kept the cards she said that she "had an overwhelming need to shop."

NO REMORSE, NO SYMPATHY

Dana displayed no sympathy for the victims. One psychologist noted that some of Dana's answers were like a robot answering in a manner they believed a normal human should.

After a hearing, Deputy District Attorney Richard Bentley wanted the death penalty. Dana pleaded insanity for all charges. But a witness came forward and stated that she saw Dana at Roberts' house on the day of her death, Dana quickly changed her plea to guilty and robbing and murdering two women as well as the attempted murder at the antique shop.

"At the end of the day," Dixon said. "Dana didn't want to die. When a witness came forward and said she saw Dana at the Roberts' house perhaps she knew that she was done for and would have been executed. Maybe she did not have enough confidence in her ability to pull off the insanity defense. So she struck a deal. She would plead guilty and avoid the death penalty."

Nonetheless, prosecutors were still unable to determine how Dana left the bloody crime scenes without a speck of blood on her or any sign of a struggle. All the clerks and waitresses spotted nothing out of the usual.

LIFE WITHOUT PAROLE

On October 16th, 1998, Dana Sue Gray was sentenced to life without parole.

"It's hard to find words to describe the atrocity in this case," Judge Patrick Magers said during Dana's sentencing. "The crimes were horrendous, callous and despicable."

Dana is currently jailed at the California Women's Prison in Chowchilla.

"She enjoyed the power," Dixon said. "She got addicted to the power she obtained while she killed people who were helpless to fight back. She liked watching them struggle. Liked having control over them before they died."

Jail has not seemed to bother Dana as she referred to her incarceration as her "county condo." She continues to pester her jailers to replicate her high-maintenance civilian lifestyle. She insists on a vegetarian diet and wants the use of a chiropractor. She has requested a mirror and has lobbied consistently for the return of her belongings.

Dana has drawn chilling clown faces, cobbling her paints together from M&M's candy coating, cherry drink mix, lipstick and and baby powder.

Her family came to visit her and brought her a pair of cheap Nike's. She refused them, wanting the high-end models.

Dana continues to thumb her nose at authorities as she sometimes sends collectibles to "murderablia" websites. She has sold her panties at $250, where she autographs them and writes in her prison identification number. She sells her hand tracing for $65 and a 'prison worn shirt', decorated with a drawing of a blue butterfly perched on a skeleton's hand.

"We can look back and say that she was simply psychotic," Dixon said. "And it is really easy to dismiss her killings as someone who was simply crazy violent and not read into it anymore than that. But in looking at the ages and gender of the victim, we can see the connection. All of her victims were old enough to be her mother. So perhaps in Dana's mind she saw her victims as substitutes for her late mother with whom had a lot of anger toward. And I mean violent, aggressive anger. So when she subdued her victims with the phone cord, she would unleash a torrent of rage, smashing them with irons, stabbing them with utility knives,bashing them over the head with wine bottles. She would attack them and have flashbacks of her battles with her Mom, doing things to the victim that she was powerless to do to her mother as a little girl."

"She was doing it all for Mommy."

HELL'S BELLE : THE TRUE STORY OF BELLE GUNNESS

LINDSAY GARRETT

A serial killer is defined as a person who commits murders three or more times. Serial killing usually takes place because of an abnormal and perverted psychological gratification. As for the murder, they can take place over the course of more than a month. There is usually a significant break between two murders, this break being called a cooling off period. However, some agencies like the FBI tend to disregard the criterion of three murders. For them, even two murders can be classified as serial killing. Usually, the serial killer acts alone. Psychological gratification is the typical motive behind serial killing but it is not the only motive. Attention seeking, anger and financial gain are other possible motives.

Throughout history, there have been a number of serial killers who acts have horrified their fellow men. The names of some such as Jack the Ripper have achieved notoriety. They have been called monsters and worse. Nonetheless, the fact remains that all of them took the lives of other human beings no matter what their reasons were.

Belle Sorenson Gunness was one who fell into this category. She was Norwegian-American and stood six feet tall and weighed more than 200 pounds. No wonder, she was rather physically strong. She ended up killing most of her boyfriends and suitors. Horrifically, she also murdered two of her daughters. It is not verified but seems very likely that she killed her two husbands and all her children on varying occasions. Her motives apparently seem to have been to collect life insurance, valuables and cash. Elimination of witnesses was another possible motive. According to reports, she has been responsible for the murders of at least 25 people over the course of several decades. Some reports claim she murdered

This is the biography of a ruthless woman whose abominable deeds earned her nicknames such as Lady Bluebeard, Hell's Belle and the Mistress of Murder Farm. She has gone down in history as one of the most prolific serial killers of America. What is surprising is that her crimes were not discovered before 1908 by which time, she had already fled leaving behind a farm full of dead bodies.

The Early Years of Belle Sorenson Gunness

The origins of one of the most notorious female American serial killers are rather murky and debatable. The majority of the biographers of Belle Sorenson Gunness have stated that she was born on the 11th of November, 1859. Her birthplace is believed to be somewhere around the lake of Selbu in the county of Sør-Trøndelag, Norway.

Belle Sorenson Gunness was christened as Brynhild Paulsdatter Størset. She was born to Paul Pedersen Størset who worked as a stonemason and his wife Berit Olsdatter. Her parents had 8 children of which she was the youngest. The family lived at a rather small cotter's farm called Størsetgjerdet located in Innbygda. Innbygda itself lies 60km away from Trondheim in a southeast direction. Trondheim is the largest city in the central region of Norway and it lies inside the Trøndelag county.

An Irish TV documentary told of a story about the early life of Belle Sorenson Gunness. Although the story is a rather common one, it has remained unverified by experts so far. As per the story, the event took place in 1877. Belle was attending a country dance even though she was pregnant. At the dance, she was attacked by a man who ended up kicking her abdomen. This caused Belle to end up miscarrying her child. As the man came from a rich family, he escaped being prosecuted by the authorities in Norway. The event changed the personality of Belle significantly according to people who knew Belle. An interesting thing to note about this story is that the man died soon after this event. The death of the man was said to have been caused by stomach cancer.

Whether this story is true or not is still up for debate. However, the fact remains that she immigrated to the United States of America. Since Belle had grown up poor and in poverty, she took service on a bigger and wealthy farm. She continued working there for 3 years so that she could accumulate enough money to pay for her fare for her trip to USA. She seems to have been emulating the example of one of her sisters, Nellie Larson. Larson had immigrated to the country earlier.

In 1881, Belle came to the United States of America. She adopted her new name as it seemed more American. In the beginning, Belle found work as a servant.

The First Victim

The thing about serial killers or even a murderer is that it is not easy to predict one. It is not always possible to identify a killer until the first murder. So far, with Belle, there has been nothing in her life to suggest that she would be capable of killing more than 25 people. However, things began to change from the year 1884.

In 1884, Belle wed Mads Ditlev Anton Sorenson in the city of Chicago, Illinois. 2 years later, the couple opened up a confectionery store. Unfortunately, the business did not become a success. Within just one year, the store burned down rather mysteriously. It was not too bad for the couple as they managed to collect the insurance. This insurance was used to pay for another home.

Some researchers believe that the couple did not have any children. However, there are investigators who have reported that Belle and Mads Sorenson had four children. They were Caroline, Axel, Myrtle and Lucy. Out of these four, Axel and Caroline died in their infancy. It has been alleged that acute colitis was responsible for their deaths. The symptoms of acute colitis include fever, diarrhea and nausea, cramping and lower abdominal pain. However, these symptoms are also displayed by a variety of poisoning. The lives of Axel and Caroline were supposedly insured. The insurance company apparently paid out.

Sorenson also had two life insurance policies to his name. On the 30th of July 1900, Sorenson was found dead. What is remarkable is that the 30th of July was also the only day on which both policies overlapped.

The first doctor who checked Sorenson believed that he had died due to strychnine poisoning. This was not the view of the family doctor of the Sorensons'. The family doctor had been treating Mads Sorenson for an enlarged heart condition. It was the belief of the family doctor that the cause of death was heart failure. Since the death did not seem to be suspicious by anyone, an autopsy was not performed. As for Belle, she told the doctor that she had only given the medicinal powders to her husband so as to make him feel better.

The very next day after the funeral of Mads Sorenson, his widow, Belle went to the insurance companies to apply for the insurance money. The relatives of Sorenson believed and even claimed that Sorenson had been poisoned by Belle so that she could collect the insurance money.

According to the surviving records, an inquest on Sorenson was ordered. However, there are no records to show whether the investigation actually went ahead. It is also not clear if the body of Sorenson was ever exhumed for the purposes of detecting arsenic as per the demands of his relatives.

Belle, on the other hand, managed to collect around $8,500 from the insurance companies. That amount would be equivalent to approximately $240,000 in 2012. Belle used the company to buy a farm located on the outskirts of the city of La Porte in the state of Indiana.

On the 13th of June, Belle and her family was included in the United States Census in the city of Chicago. As per the census, Belle was recorded as the mother of 4 children out of whom only 2 were living. They were Myrtle and Lucy, then 3 and 1 years old. The census also mentions an adopted girl of 10 years. She was identified as possibly being Morgan Couch. However, it seems that she was apparently called Jennie Olsen later.

It seems very likely that Belle Sorenson killed her husband for the sake of money. However, there is no proof about it. Whether she killed her two children or not is also up for debate. Even if she did, she got away with it.

The First Murder Suspicion

Belle Sorenson moved to La Porte in Indiana in 1901. She bought a house on McClung Road. According to reports, it seems that the carriage and the boat houses were burnt down completely within a short period of time after Belle had bought the property.

More important is what happened as Belle Sorenson was moving to La Porte from Chicago. During her move, she became acquainted with Peter Gunness. Peter was not only born in Norway but he was also a recent widower. They decided to get married and the ceremony took place on the 1st of April, 1902.

Just one week after the wedding, the infant daughter of Peter Gunness died. The cause of death remained uncertain but it was known that she was alone in the house with Belle. Again, it has remained unclear whether Belle was responsible for her death even though it does seem very likely.

Peter Gunness himself met his death in December 1902 in what was called a tragic death. Apparently, Peter was trying to reach for his slippers which was located close to the kitchen stove. It was at that moment when he got scalded with brine. This was the report by Belle

Gunness after Peter's death. However, Belle later claimed that it was actually a part of a grinding machine for sausages that fell on Peter's head from a high shelf. The part caused a head injury that turned fatal.

Belle Gunness managed to get $3,000 out of the death of her husband but some sources claim that the amount was around $4,000. Be that as it may, the people of the locality did not believe that Peter Gunness could have been so clumsy so as to die in such a way. He was known in the locality to be a hog butcher with considerable experience. Additionally, Peter had been running a hog farm in the La Porte property. The district coroner was called to review the case. He unequivocally announced the fact that Peter had been murdered. A coroner's jury was also convened by the district coroner in order to look into the case.

Even though the situation looked bleak, Belle Gunness managed to somehow successfully convince the investigators and jury that she was completely innocent and that she had got nothing to do with her husband's death.

What is interesting is that Belle Gunness made no mention of her pregnancy at the time. She was already carrying Peter's son who was born in May 1903. The son was named Philip. By revealing her pregnancy, sympathy might have been inspired but Gunness did not do so for some reason.

Approximately a year after Peter's death, his brother, Gust came to take away his older daughter. The girl, called Swanhild, was taken away to

Wisconsin. As such, she became the only child to have survived being with Belle Gunness.

For the next few years after Peter's death, Belle maintained a low profile. Keep in mind that she may have already been responsible for the deaths of two husbands and three children. According to psychology, it is not easy for a serial killer to give up their ways. Belle Gunness, the serial killer, would soon return and she did.

Her next murder took place in 1906. Late that year, Belle informed her neighbors that Jennie Olsen, her foster daughter, had joined a Lutheran College located in Los Angeles. However, some of her neighbors were told that Jennie had joined a finishing school meant for young ladies. In reality, Jennie was murdered by Belle. Her body would be found buried in the La Porte property later.

Belle continued to run her La Porte farm from 1903 to 1906. Another turning point in her life came in 1907 when she employed Ray Lamphere as her only farm hand to help her with the chores at the farm. Ray Lamphere would go on to play an important role in her story.

The Years of the Suitors

In 1907, Belle Gunness, as she was known after her marriage to Peter Gunness, hired a man called Ray Lamphere to work as a farmhand at her farm. However, this was not the only major decision she took during this time. Her other decision would have far reaching consequences and certainly paved her way to becoming a full-fledged serial killers.

Belle Gunness began to place advertisements in the matrimonial columns in newspapers to attract men who would later go on to become her victims. She chose not only the daily newspapers of Chicago but also the daily newspapers of other major cities in the Midwest.

The advertisement mentioned the following points. A beautiful widow with a large farm in La Porte, Indiana, wants to make the acquaintance of a gentleman. The gentleman should be well provided as the widow wants to join fortunes. The gentleman should be willing to come for a personal visit.

On hindsight, there are quite a few points about the advertisement that stands out such as the need for wealth and a personal visit. Suffice to say, quite a number of men responded to the advertisement placed by Belle Gunness. Of course, they were men of means as well.

One of the men who appeared at Gunness' farm was John Moe. He had come from Elbow Lake in Minnesota. He arrived with over $1,000. The purpose of the money was to help Gunness pay off the mortgage according to what he told the neighbors. Gunness introduced John Moe as her cousin to the neighbors. In just a week of his coming to the farm, John Moe disappeared.

Another of these suitors was George Anderson. He hailed from Tarkio in Missouri. He was also an immigrant from Norway. During dinner, Gunness broached the subject of her mortgage with Anderson. Anderson was willing to pay for the mortgage but only if they ended up getting married. That night, Anderson was sleeping in the guest room. He woke suddenly only to find Belle Gunness standing over him and peering into Anderson's eyes while holding a candle. The expression on Gunness' face was murderous and highly sinister. Anderson was so shocked that he yelled loudly. That seemed to have surprised Gunness who proceeded to run away from the room immediately without saying a single word.

Anderson felt very uncomfortable and terrified. He seemed to have guessed at the intentions of murder that Gunness had. As such, he got up from the bed and got dressed. He then fled Gunness' house without even saying goodbye. Even as he was running away, he still kept one eye over his shoulder. He was afraid that Gunness would come after him. Once he reached the station in La Porte, he took the first train going to Missouri. He did not bother to come back for his belongings or speak to Belle again. Anderson remains to be the only suitor to have escaped the LaPorte Black Widow.

Anderson wasn't the last of Gunness' suitors however. There was Ole B. Budsberg from Iola in Wisconsin. He was an elderly widower. The last time he was seen alive was on the 6th of April, 1907 at the La Porte Savings Bank. There, Budsberg mortgaged his land in Wisconsin and signed a deed. He got several thousand dollars in cash as a result of the transaction. Oscar and Mathew Budsberg, his sons, did not even know that Ole Budsberg had gone to visit Belle Gunness. Once they learned of his destination, the sons contacted Gunness. Belle replied promptly and stated that she had never seen Ole Budsberg.

Throughout 1907, many middle-aged men came to Gunness' farm. They seemingly appeared for brief visits and then disappeared. One of her last visitors was Andrew Helgelien. Helgelien was a bachelor farmer with whom Gunness started corresponding some time in December 1907. He came from Aberdeen, South Dakota. Previous to his arrival, Helgelien had exchanged many letters with Belle Gunness. Her last letter to him is what prompted his arrival. Helgelien seems to have been overwhelmed with the contents of the letter. It was dated 13th of January, 1908 and was found later at the Helgelien farm.

The letter ended with the words, 'Come prepared to stay forever'. In hindsight, that sentence seemed to have come true.

Helgelien visited Gunness in January, 1908 as the response to the letter. Helgelien carried with him a check for the sum of $2,900, which was his savings that had been drawn from Helgelien's local bank. A few days after his arrival, Helgelien and Guinness were seen at the Savings Bank, La Porte, where he deposited the check.

Helgelien disappeared a few days later after that event. On the other hand, Gunness visited the Savings Bank twice to make deposits of $500 and $700. It was also during this time that Belle Gunness began to have problems with Ray Lamphere, her farm hand.

In March 1908, Belle Gunness began to correspond with Lon Townsend who worked as a horse dealer and farmer in the city of Topeka in Kansas. Several letters were exchanged between them. He had been invited to visit her but he decided to wait till spring before he visited. By the time he was ready to visit, there was a fire at the Gunness farm. As such he could not visit. Another person who escaped this face was a man from the state of Arkansas. He, too, had to cancel his visit due to the fire. Another person was Bert Albert. Allegedly, Gunness had promised to marry him. However, the marriage was called off as Bert Albert did not have much wealth.

There was certainly no shortage of suitors. However, none of them, being as lucky as Anderson, left the farm of Belle Gunness alive. By the time of Anderson, Gunness had started to order huge trunks. These trunks were to be delivered to Gunness' home. Clyde Sturgis, a hack driver, was responsible for many of these deliveries from La Porte. Later, Sturgis remarked as to how Gunness was capable of lifting up those huge trunks as if they were 'boxes of marshmallows' and tossed them over her shoulders and took them inside the house herself. This goes on to show how strong Gunness was.

It was noticed that Belle kept the shutters of the house closed irrespective of whether it was day or night. Belle kept mostly to herself. Additionally, farmers who travelled by the farm at night often noticed her digging around in the hog pen with a shovel.

The Story of Ray Lamphere

Ray Lamphere was hired by Belle Gunness to work in her farm as a farmhand. However, Lamphere fell in love with Gunness deeply. In fact, he was willing to perform any chore for Gunness irrespective of how dirty or gruesome the task was.

With all the men visiting Belle Gunness for her hand in marriage, Ray Lamphere began to become very jealous of them. He began to cause scenes with Gunness. On the 3rd of February 1908, Gunness fired Lamphere from his job. Within a short period of time from that date, Gunness visited the courthouse of La Porte County and presented herself. There, she declared that Ray Lamphere, her former employee, had lost his mind. As such, he was a menace and danger to the public.

Somehow, Belle Gunness managed to convince the local authorities for holding a sanity hearing for Ray Lamphere. Of course, Lamphere was found and declared to be sane and, therefore, released. A few days later, Gunness visited the sheriff. She complained that Lamphere was visiting her at the farm and arguing. She mentioned that he seemed to pose a threat to her family. As such, Lamphere was arrested on the charges of trespassing.

That did not stop Lamphere from returning to the farm again and again. However, Gunness managed to drive him away. Lamphere even began to make threats, thinly disguised though. In one particular instance, Lamphere had confided to William Slater, a farmer, that Helgelian would not bother him any more as they had 'fixed him for keeps'. By that time, it was believed that Helgelian had vanished from La Porte a long time ago.

On the other hand, the brother of Andrew Helgelian, Asle Helgelian, became disturbed and concerned when Andrew did not come back home. He wrote to Gunness and asked if she knew anything about the whereabouts of his brother. Belle replied that Andrew was not at her farm. She also mentioned that Andrew might have possibly gone to Norway to visit his relatives. This did not sit well with Asle who said that he could not believe that Andrew would do such a thing. More importantly, Asle believed that Andrew was still somewhere in the vicinity of La Porte. It was, after all, the last place that Andrew had been seen and heard. Belle Gunness decided to brazen it out. She wrote back to Asle informing that he could come and search for his brother if he wanted. She would even help him conduct a search. However, Gunness also cautioned him saying that a search for missing people was an expensive task. As such, Asle should be ready to pay for Gunness' efforts if she had to get involved in the search. Asle Helgelian would certainly come to La Porte but that visit would take place in May 1908. By then, things had changed.

In the meantime, Lamphere became a danger to Belle Gunness. Additionally, Asle Helgelian seemed to be making inquiries which could end with her being sent to the gallows. Belle Gunness realized that something had to be done.

Belle contacted M.E. Leliter, a lawyer in the city of La Porte. She told him that she was afraid for her life as well as that of her children. She stated that Ray Lamphere had threatened to kill her and even burn down her house. Belle wanted the lawyer to create a will just in case Ray Lamphere managed to carry out his threats. The later did comply with the wishes of Gunness and drew up the will. According to the will, the entire estate of Gunness would be left to her children.

After concluding her business at the lawyer's office, Belle Gunness visited one of the banks in La Porte that held that mortgage for her property. She paid off the mortgage. However, Belle Gunness failed to visit the police and inform them about the threats to her life by Belle Gunness. It was only later that it was realized that she had intentionally not visited the police. After all, there had never been any threats from Ray Lamphere. All of the talk at the lawyer's office was mere ruse and the setting up of an elaborate plan that would come into effect only later.

The Fire at the Gunness Farm

In the wee hours of 28th April, 1908, Joe Maxson woke to the smell of smoke in his room. Joe had been hired as a replacement for Ray Lamphere back in February 1908. That morning, he was sleeping in his room on the second floor of the house belonging to Belle Gunness.

On that morning, Joe opened the door to the hall only to find it engulfed in flames. He screamed out the names of Belle Gunness as well as that of her children. However, he did not get any response. He shut the door and decided to jump out from the window of his room on the second story in just his underwear. He barely survived the fire which had by that time nearly covered the entire house. Maxson ran to the town in order to get help. Unfortunately, by the time the old fashioned fire truck arrived at the farm, it was already dawn and the house was nothing more than a pile of smoldering ruins.

In the midst of the ruins, four bodies were found. One of the bodies belonged to a woman. It could not be immediately confirmed if that body belonged to Belle Gunness as the head was missing. In fact, the head was never found. The 3 other bodies belonged to the children of Belle and they were in their beds when found. Was this the tragic end of Belle Gunness? Not quite.

County Sheriff Smutzer had come to hear about the alleged threats given by Ray Lamphere somehow. After taking one look at the scene in the farm, he decided to hunt for the farmhand. The lawyer, Leliter, also came forward and told about his meeting with Belle Gunness. He mentioned how Gunness was afraid that Lamphere had threatened her. He told that Gunness had mentioned among the threats that Lamphere would also burn her house down.

As things stood, the future seemed bleak for Lamphere and he did not do much to improve his cause. When Sheriff Smutzer found him,

Lamphere was reported to have asked if Gunness and her family got out all right. What is surprising is that he asked the question even before the sheriff said anything. Only then was he informed of the fire.

However, Lamphere denied having any connection with the affair. He claimed that he was not present when the conflagration erupted. This proved to be false when a youth called John Solyem came forward. John claimed that he had been near the house and that he saw Ray coming down the road moments before the fire. Lamphere alleged that the boy was lying. However, Solyem claimed that Lamphere had found him hiding behind the bushes and that he was threatened by Ray.

The Investigation and the Discovery

The headless woman proved to be a source of consternation for the residents of La Porte. It did not seem to be the body of Belle Gunness after all. A neighboring farmer of Gunness, C. Christofferson declared that the remains were not that of Gunness. L. Nicholson, a farmer, and Mrs. Austin Cutler, also said the same thing. Some old friends of Gunness from Chicago, Mr. Sigward Olsen and Mrs. May Olander examined the body and said that it did not belong to Gunness.

The remains were then measured by doctors. After making allowances for the missing head and neck, they found out that the corpse could only belong to a woman with a height of 5 feet three inches and a maximum weight of 150 pounds. Neighbors and friends were fairly certain that it could not have been Gunness. Measurements were also taken from the stores where Gunness bought her clothes.

A comparison between the two sets of measurements proved that the body could not belong to Belle Gunness. Another crucial fact came to light by Dr. J. Meyers who examined the corpse's internal organs. He discovered that the organs contained strychnine in lethal doses.

It was during this juncture that Asle Helgelien made his appearance in La Porte. He informed Sheriff Smutzer about his suspicions that Gunness was responsible for the disappearance of his brother. However, it was the statement of Joe Maxson that spurred the Sheriff into action. Maxson informed the Sheriff that he had to carry loads of dust into a big area that was meant for feeding the hogs. That area was fenced by high wire and contained a number of deep depressions. The holes were covered by dirt and Gunness had said that they contained rubbish.

With this information, Sheriff Smutzer had to take a few men to the farm and start digging. On the 3rd of May 1908, the first body was unearthed. It was discovered to be the body of Jennie Olson who had vanished in December 1906. It was followed by the corpses of two unidentified children. Later, Andrew Helgelien's body was unearthed. More and more bodies began to be discovered.

The Aftermath

On the 22nd of May 1908, Ray Lamphere was arrested on the charges of murder and arson and tried. He denied these charges. However, the subsequent investigation found him guilty of arson. However, he was acquitted of murder as the body was proved not to be that of Belle Gunness. He was sentenced to serve 20 years at the State Prison on the 26th of November, 1908. On the 30th of December, 1909, Lamphere died of tuberculosis.

On the 14th of January, 1910, the clergyman, Rev. E.A. Schell, assigned to comfort the dying Lamphere came forward with an astonishing confession. In the confession, Lamphere admitted to the crimes of Gunness and also swore that the woman was still alive. Before his death, he confessed to the reverend as well as to Harry Meyers, a fellow convict, that he had never murdered any person. However, he did mention that he had helped Belle Gunness bury her victims. He mentioned how Gunness went about her killings.

Lamphere's confession also cleared up the mystery of the headless corpse found in the Gunness home. According to his statement, the woman was lured from Chicago by Gunness under the pretension of offering her a job as a housekeeper. The woman was decapitated and dressed to look like Gunness. As for the children, they were smothered to death.

After setting the house on fire, Gunness was supposed to have met Lamphere. However, she betrayed him and left via the open fields instead of meeting him at the road. By Lamphere's account, Gunness had murdered 42 men and taken money from them. By the end of her career, she had accumulated more than $250,000 which would be $6.3 million in 2012.

At the end, the true fate of Belle Sorenson Gunness remains a mystery. As it happens with such cases, people have claimed having seen her over the years none of which could be confirmed. On the 5th of November, 2007, the headless body was unearthed in order to determine once and for all if it actually belonged to Belle Gunness with the help of DNA analysis. However, there was a lack of DNA to compare it to. As such, the mystery of her end continues.

The List of Victims at the Gunness Farm

There were many bodies found at the farm owned by Belle Gunness. In fact, there were so many bodies that a sluice had to be created to separate the bodies from the dirt.

Positive Identifications:
Ole B. Budsberg
Henry Gurholdt
Thomas Lindboe
John Moe
Olaf Svenherud
Olaf Svenherud

Possible Victims
These are plausible victims who may or may not have met their demise at the hands of Belle Sorenson Gunness.
Herman Konitzer

William Mingay
George Berry
Christie Hilkven
Charles Edman
John H. McJunkin
Chares Neiburg
Henry Bizge
Tonnes Peterson Lien
T.J. Tie

CAROL SUMNER

DINA LIVINGSTONE

When James "Reggie" and Carol Sumner moved to Jacksonville, Florida for their retirement, they had visions of good health and happiness. They never thought that their overnight invitation to long-time South Carolina neighbor, Tiffany Cole, would end up the way it did; With the Sumner couple being buried alive.

Reggie and Carol Sumner were high school sweethearts in North Charleston, South Carolina. They were the kind of couple that everyone envied as they walked down the hall. Unfortunately, their lives pulled them in different directions. Reggie decided to serve his country in the navy. After finishing his tour, he got married and landed a job with the railroad. Carol also married and became a devoted mother, however, her first marriage ended in divorce, and her second nearly killed her. In 1987, after years of abuse, her husband at the time shot her seven times in their home before driving away and turning the gun on himself. Her daughter, Rhonda Alford, just ten years old at that time, spent almost a year helping her mother recover from her wounds. She had to help her bathe, dress, and take care of the house. After taking eight years to fully recover, Carol went back to work as soon as she was able. For over twenty-five years she was a civil servant at the Citadel and the Charleston Air Force Base. She also worked a second job at night at a Belk department store, among other jobs she would take when needed. She did whatever she had to in order to make ends meet. Shortly after her recovery, she found out that the blood transfusion she had received during her previous trauma had given her Hepatitis C. She was angry because she felt as though she could not escape her late ex-husband, but she refused to let it ruin her life. She soon started a new job at a cable company and it was during this time that her life finally changed for the better. Nearly forty years after they'd left high school, a chance encounter brought Carol and Reggie together again. One night in 2000, a phone call was made to the cable company where Carol was working, which she received. After talking with the customer Carol and learning his name, she realized that he also sounded just like the Reggie she remembered. So she asked him if he was the same Reggie Sumner who attended Garrett High school in South Charleston. It was. They decided that they should get together after not seeing each other in so long. This time, though they were inseparable. Like "teenagers in love", a quick courtship led to love and then marriage in 2001 with a ceremony at Carol's home in West Ashley. Carol's daughter has said of Reggie "he was just a very gentle, kind and giving spirit. You could not ask for a better friend, husband or stepfather." Eventually, after retiring, the couple decided to move from South Carolina to Jacksonville, Florida. Reggie had previously bought a house during his days working for CSX railroad and as he was a "brittle" diabetic in frail health, he thought he would be more comfortable in the warmer climate. Carol agreed. "She only went down there to honor her husband," Rhonda said. Before moving, they decided to sell their Chevrolet Lumina to the stepdaughter of a friend who lived down the street, Tiffany Cole. They allowed her to make payments on the car to help her out and she agreed, often driving down to Jacksonville with friends to make those payments. Tiffany and the Sumners became friends and Tiffany would often spend the night at their house when she and her friends went down south. A pleasant girl on the outside, the Sumners had no idea what Tiffany could really be like.

Tiffany Ann Cole was born on December 3, 1981, to her sixteen-year-old mother, Shirley Duncan. Her biological father was in jail. She had no male role model to look up to or who could offer her protection the way a father should. Her mother had a boyfriend, but he was beyond cruel and especially loved to torment Tiffany. At one point, she had a puppy which her stepdad threw against a wall, breaking its neck right in front of her. He was abusive verbally as well as physically and Tiffany claims that as a young girl, he began to molest her, beginning around age eight. As a young teenager, she turned to alcohol and drugs to deal with the pain. In high school, Tiffany was a student who participated in cheerleading and played the flute. She was also a girl scout member but eventually the alcohol and drugs took over her life and she quit her programs and dropped out of school. At one point she fell in love with a boy with severe epilepsy, who ended up breaking her heart and since the only example of love from a man came from an abusive stepfather, this breakup reinforced the belief that she should expect to be treated badly and let down by men. She began looking for love in all the wrong places. In May of 2005, during a six-month period of prostitution, Tiffany ran into a man by the name of Michael Jackson. They were drawn to each other right away and began to get high and sleep together.

Michael James Jackson, born May 12, 1982, had a significant criminal history beginning in childhood. Born to a drug-addicted mother, he was mostly raised by his grandmother. He had multiple felony convictions but only for things like fraud and theft. After meeting Tiffany and becoming close, they took a road trip, first going to Myrtle Beach, then driving to Jacksonville, Florida, where they would be staying with Michael's best friend, Alan Wade. Born May 22, 1987, Alan and Michael had known each other for just over a year. When Tiffany and Michael arrived in Florida, they stayed at Alan's mom's house. After just a few days, though, she kicked them out because she was tired of the loud noises and constant partying. With nowhere else to go and with all their money spent on the nights of drinking and partying, Tiffany remembered that the Sumners lived nearby. The three friends showed up at their doorstep and explained what had happened. The couple was very happy to see Tiffany and invited her and her friends to stay the night. While they were chatting and catching up, Carol mentioned how worried they had been about their house in North Carolina not selling. There was no need to worry, however, because not only did their property sell, but they had also made a $99,000 profit. It was this general statement to a long-time neighbor that sealed the Sumner's fate.

It's difficult to know just whose idea it was to rob the Sumner's. Some say it was both Tiffany and Michael, while others say it was Michael who was the plan maker and master manipulator. Either way, a plan was hatched to rob and kill the loving couple. At some point in June, Alan had contacted his friend, Bruce Nixon Jr., and told him of a plan to rob someone. No other details were given. Then on July 6th, Alan called Bruce, born May 9th, 1987, and asked him if he would be interested in joining the others in digging a hole. Bruce agreed and stole four shovels from his neighborhood. The other three friends drove to Bruce's house in a rented Mazda RX-8 that Tiffany had rented in South Carolina. The group drove around hoping to find a perfectly remote place for the hole to be dug. Alan asked Bruce if he knew of any good places to which Bruce responded that he did. He took them into Georgia, to a wooded area just over the state line. Leaving the car parked on the road, the group walked through the wooded area into a clearing where they began to dig a hole while Tiffany held a flashlight. It was approximately four feet deep and six feet square. Upon completion of the hole, they left the shovels and went back to the car. It was here that Alan asked Michael if Bruce could join in on their robbery plan. Michael agreed. The foursome drove back to Alan's house but his mother would not allow Michael in as she believed him to be a bad influence on her son. Over the next couple of days, it was Tiffany's job to remain in contact with Carol and Reggie in order to gain information from them about their plans and whereabouts. The foursome also secretly watched the house in order to figure out the Sumner's routine. It was unclear yet as to whether or not the group would enter the home while the couple was gone or if they would simply go in with the couple there. It was ultimately decided that they would enter the home while the couple was there so that they could get their financial information and the means to access their accounts. Michael said that he would kill the victims by injecting them with a lethal dose of their medications. He then promised that the four friends would split the money they received from the Sumner's accounts, each receiving about $50,000. They began making preparations for their plan. Just after midnight on July 8th, 2005, Michael, Tiffany, and Alan went to Wal-Mart and purchased disposable rubber gloves. On the evening of the murders, they went to an Office Depot, where Tiffany bought duct tape and a large roll of plastic wrap. Last, they bought a toy gun that shot plastic pellets.

Around 10pm., on July 8th, 2005, Tiffany drove the other three group members to the Sumner's house in the Mazda. Herself and Michael remained in the car while Alan and Bruce went up to the door. They had the duct tape and toy gun and both were wearing the plastic gloves. After Carol answered the door, Bruce and Alan told her that they were having car trouble and asked if they could use their phone. Carol said of course they could and invited them in. As soon as the boys entered the home, Alan pulled the phone cord out of the wall. Bruce pointed the gun at the couple. Alan grabbed Reggie around the neck and pushed him down into a chair. They told the couple that they wanted credit and debit cards and any other financial information. Carol began pleading with the boys not to hurt them. Bruce took the couple into a spare bedroom where he used duct tape to bind their legs and hands and to cover their mouths and eyes. Alan sent a text message to Michael, informing him that everything was under control. Michael then also entered the home and he and Alan began searching for financial information. They saw a pile of mail and financial statements which they put into a plastic bag. They spotted Reggie's prized coin collection and took that too. Michael told the other two to take the couple into the garage at which point they put them into the trunk of the Lincoln Town car. Tiffany went into the house and grabbed some of their belongings, put them into a bag and took the bag with her to the Mazda. Following the plan, both cars headed towards the gravesite, stopping only once to put gas in the Lincoln. Upon arrival at the site, Michael opened the trunk and apparently began screaming when he saw that the duct tape had become loose and the couple had worked the tape off. It had been over 100 degrees in the trunk. Sweat had caused the tape to loosen. They had also taken the tape off their eyes and were huddled together. Michael ordered Bruce to tape them up again, which he did. Alan then attempted to back up the car to the edge of the grave but, unable to do so, Bruce took over. Michael then sent Bruce up the road to wait with Tiffany at the Mazda. While still alive, the Sumners were taken out of the trunk and pushed into the hole. It is unclear as to who actually did the burying because Alan and Michael each blamed the other. Somehow, Michael ended up getting the personal identification number of the Sumner's bank account. Reports differ on whether he obtained this information from somewhere in the house or if Carol told him the number while being threatened to be buried alive. According to one documentary, Carol had gotten the tape off her mouth again when in the hole. Michael was telling them that if they didn't give up their PIN, they would die, at which point Carol yelled it out. It didn't seem to matter either way though because they continued to shovel dirt onto the scared couple.

After filling the hole, Alan and Michael put the shovels back into the trunk of the Lincoln and drove it up the road to where Tiffany and Bruce were waiting with the Mazda. The four of them drove to Sanderson, Florida, where they abandoned the Lincoln after wiping it clean of fingerprints. They then drove back to Jacksonville where they immediately went to an ATM and withdrew money from the Sumner's account, before retiring to a hotel. Alan and Tiffany went to another Wal-Mart where they purchased more latex gloves as well as bleach. They returned to the Sumner's home in order to clean up any evidence. They also stole a computer. Bruce stayed with the group for another day and then went home, but Alan remained with Michael and Tiffany who returned to South Carolina, where Tiffany rented two hotel rooms; one for herself and Michael and one for Alan. It should be noted that after returning home, Bruce went to a party with a plastic bag filled with different medications. At one point he announced that he had found a new job murdering people. He stated that he had buried people alive and killed them without mentioning the involvement of anyone else.

On the morning of July 10th, Carol's daughter, Rhonda, decided to report to police the fact that she hadn't been able to get hold of her mother for a few days. Since they kept in touch on a regular basis and spoke every couple days, it was highly unusual for her mother to not return her calls. The next day, the Jacksonville Sheriff's Office (JSO) went to the Sumner's home. The back door of the house was unlocked and in the kitchen there dirty after-dinner plates, which was also highly unusual for the couple. The JSO began to investigate the financial accounts of the couple and they found that large amounts of money had been withdrawn within a short time frame. Video footage from the ATM machines that the group had used showed Michael's face and the silver Mazda in the background. On July 12th, after Rhonda made a plea on local TV networks for the safe return of her parents, the Sheriff's office received a phone call from someone posing as Reggie Sumner. Dispatch contacted Detective David Meacham of the Sheriff's office and put the caller through.

Meacham: Where are you at?

Michael: We're in Delaware right now

Meacham: And what city is that in?

Michael: It's in Corpus

Meacham: Corpus, Delaware?

Michael: Yes

However, the town of Corpus, Delaware does not exist. Next, Tiffany came on the phone posing as Carol.

Meacham: Is this Carol?

Tiffany: Yes, sir, it is.

Meacham: Okay. This is Detective Meacham from the Sheriff's office. How are you doing tonight?

Tiffany: I was sleeping

Meacham: I understand. I understand you have some health problems

Tiffany: Mmhmm

Meacham: Okay. Any other problems?

Tiffany: I'm really tired right now

Meacham: What kind of problems do you have?

Tiffany: Cancer

Meacham: Cancer?

Tiffany: Mmhmm

The detective called Rhonda into the station so that she could listen to the taped conversation. She confirmed that the people posing as the Sumners were definitely not Carol and Reggie. The main reason for the call was to ensure everyone that the Sumners were alive and well and because the bank accounts had been frozen. They asked the detectives to reinstate the accounts, which they did so that they could track the money in order to locate the perpetrators. They also had the phone number from which Michael had called. Using this information, they were able to find that the phone was registered to Michael and that a call had been placed to a car rental agency in Charleston. They also learned that the cell had been used near the Sumner's home the night of the murders. Detective Meacham contacted the rental company and was told that the car had been rented to a Tiffany Cole and that it was overdue. Using the rental car's GPS system, they were able to find that the car had also been near the Sumner's residence during the time of the abduction. Using the cell phone trace, the car's GPS and the photos of Michael at different ATMs, police were able to locate the general whereabouts of the three murderers. On July 14th, with help from Tiffany's brother, who was on probation and threatened with jail, police raided a Best Western hotel in Charleston and arrested Tiffany

Cole, Alan Wade, and Michael Jackson. Bruce Nixon was also picked up at his home in Florida.

While Tiffany, Michael, and Alan refused to cooperate with law enforcement, Bruce appeared to have some semblance of a conscience because he broke down and admitted to the crimes right away. He also agreed to lead police to the burial site. For the first time in TV history, documentary footage showed Bruce and detectives at the grave site where Bruce broke down in sobs. Excavation of the site began the next day. The victims were found fully clothed in a crouching position. Reggie had somehow broken his tape and was holding Carol's hand. There was two feet of dirt over their heads. With ten years of homicide under his belt, Detective Meacham said it was one of the saddest and most horrible things he had ever seen. The medical examiner determined that both Reggie and Carol were alive in the hole before they were buried. Their nostrils, mouths, throats, esophagi, and trachea had fine sprays of dirt in them, which indicated that they had inhaled it. They died from mechanical asphyxiation and smothering, caused by the dirt covering their heads while compressing their chests. She said it was the worst case of asphyxiation she'd ever seen. It was "horrendous."

At some point while in jail, but unaware that Bruce had come clean, Michael's grandmother called him.

Grandma: Michael, listen to me and don't say a word. You're in the newspaper. All over the newspaper yesterday and today

Michael: For what?

Grandma: Murder

Michael: What?!

Grandma: Murder. 'Bodies ID'd as former South Carolina couple James and Carol Sumner. Bail was denied for 18-year-old Bruce Nixon of Florida who was arrested and charged with murder, home invasion, robbery, and kidnapping.' He took them to the grave site and everything

Michael: Oh my God. Are you kidding me?

Grandma: It's right here in today's paper

Michael: Bruce took them to the f*****g spot. The f****r showed them where the spot was at?

Grandma: Yes, dear

Michael: *starts panting* Bruce just killed us all

Bruce Nixon told detectives everything that had happened and agreed to testify on behalf of the prosecution. He wasn't sentenced until after he testified against the other three group members, but in the end, he received 45 years for each victim, currently being served concurrently at Century Correctional Institution in Florida. Alan Wade was tried first.

Michael Jackson was the first to be tried. Testifying on his own behalf, Michael stated that the plan was only to rob the Sumners and that it was not going to involve murder. He said that Alan and Bruce went into the house and when they came out they drove off in the Lincoln which he then followed. He claims he had no idea that Reggie and Carol were in the trunk. According to Michael, when they arrived at the hole in Georgia, it was Alan and Bruce who told him where to park and to bring them a flashlight. It was when he arrived at the burial site that he heard Carol moan. He then stated that he questioned what the other two were doing before returning to the Mazda to wait. He did admit to impersonating Reggie. Bruce testified that Michael had been the ringleader and was the one who orchestrated everything. After stepping down from the witness stand, Carol's daughter, Rhonda, said of Bruce, "I just wanted to hug him. He is a murderer, but in the end, he did the right thing." It was that testimony that she believed sealed Michael's fate because he was found guilty of first degree murder, robbery, and kid-napping, and sentenced to death for each murder. He is currently on death row in Florida.

Alan was next to be tried. Two witnesses who were not identified gave victim impact statements during the penalty phase. Alan's lawyer then called six of their own witnesses to testify including Bruce Nixon,

Alan's mom and sister, the mother of a friend, his middle school principal, and his youth pastor. Overall, the witnesses testified that Alan's parents divorced when he was eight and his father disappeared from his life. His mother took him to church regularly and as a kid, he was kind, smart, and well-behaved. After the divorce, his mother was unable to spend a lot of time with him because she had to work a lot to support them. When he was in his teens, his mother had a bout with breast cancer. By his early teens, he began to use drugs. In the sixth grade, he was involuntarily committed to a 72-hour hold because of a drug related incident. When he was sixteen, his mom had to take him out of school or be arrested for his truancy. The next year, his mother kicked him out of the house in an attempt at tough love because his drug use was becoming worse. In 2004 Alan introduced her to Michael, whom she immediately saw as a bad influence on him. Since his arrest and before his trial, Alan had apparently become a model prisoner, obtained his G.E.D and tutored other inmates in math. Nothing seemed to sway the jury, however, because he was found guilty on all counts and voted eleven-to-one to receive the death penalty. He is also currently on death row in Florida.

Tiffany was the last to be tried. Her lawyer argued that she wasn't a major participant in the crimes. He said that she was under the control of her boyfriend Michael, and that he was the mastermind. Tiffany claimed that she believed the crime would only constitute a simple theft and that she didn't knowingly participate in the robberies, kidnapping or murders. She insisted that she did not know that Reggie and Carol were in the trunk of the Lincoln until they arrived at the burial site. The circuit judge, Michael Weatherby did not see it that way, stating that it was she who held the flashlight during the digging of the grave and was there when they were bound and placed in the trunk. He also noted that she was the one who purchased the duct tape and gloves and later pawned the jewelry and computer they had stolen. "She was thoroughly involved," Weatherby stated. "She knew exactly what she was doing and participated without hesitation." It was noted as well that she was the only one of the four who had previously known the Sumners. During the penalty phase, the prosecution called two of the victim's family members who gave impact statements. The defense attorney then called up witnesses who testified that Tiffany was of good character. Three of those witnesses were correctional officers who stated that Tiffany had been no trouble in jail and did not cause any problems. A psychiatrist, Dr. Earnest Miller, testified that she suffered from poly-substance and alcohol abuse, chronic depression, and a personality disorder. He also stated that she had witnessed abuse to family members and had been sexually abused herself by her stepfather. On the other hand, he testified that Tiffany was competent and thus he could not support a plea of insanity. Finally, he stated that she knew right from wrong and had a high average IQ. In the end, Tiffany was also found guilty of all charges and sentenced to death by a 9-3 vote. Upon hearing her fate, she bowed her head and turned to her mother, mouthing the words "I love you". Her lawyer, Quentin Till, said she had been ready for the decision. He visited her in jail that week. "I told her to be strong," he said. "...I still see her being utilized and manipulated by Michael Jackson." Revis Sumner, Reggie's brother, said that Tiffany has since written to the family, asking for forgiveness. He says he has forgiven her, but that doesn't mean she shouldn't suffer for her actions. The Reverend Jean Clark, Reggie's sister has said, "I pray for Tiffany. I pray for all of them. I'm grieved that these four young people have wasted their lives." Chief Assistant State Attorney, Jay Plotkin, who tried all four cases said, "All of these defendants got exactly what they deserved. Justice was done." After the sentences were given and the trials were over, Reggie's son, Frederick Hallock, said, "You expect some sort of closure or some sort of good feeling when the verdict is read, but it didn't seem to help much. I just know they didn't deserve this." Currently, Tiffany is one of only five women on Florida's death row. At the time of her sentence, she was the sole woman there.

Tiffany, Michael, and Alan all filed appeals after their trials, citing multiple issues. All three were denied and their sentences were upheld. Recently, in 2015, Tiffany filed another appeal, asking for a new trial. She claims that her defense lawyers were ineffective and that she should not have been convicted of first-degree murder since she did not actually bury the bodies herself. But according to Florida law, it doesn't matter who actually committed the murder. Just knowing that it was going to happen is enough to warrant a guilty verdict. At her original trial Tiffany said, "But please remember I didn't do this. I am not the monster that created this, but I regret meeting him," referring to Michael. Upon hearing that Tiffany was asking for a new trial, Reggie's sister, Jean had this to say: "Most people are going to try to come back with something like that after the fact, because they're going to try to find a loophole and get off. But justice has a voice, and justice has to be served." And the thought of going through another trial breaks her heart. "I have family members that are still not the same and never will be the same. In fact, I don't like to involve them too much into things like this, because they can't deal with it."

In 2014, Alan Wade also filed an appeal for a new trial, citing that his lawyers did not do a good job of representing him. His appellate lawyers said that his original defense lawyers barely met with him before the trial and didn't interview witnesses prior to putting them on the stand. They also cited the lack of objections to supposedly questionable evidence. In December 2014, it was decided by the Supreme Court of Florida that his conviction be upheld.

Previous to that, Michael Jackson filed an appeal for a new trial, stating that his lawyers were also ineffective. As with Alan's trial, Michael claims that his lawyers did not make objections to certain evidence when there was clearly an objection to be made. The judge did allow an appeal hearing for his concerns and at the close of the hearing, Michael was allowed to make a statement. It went as follows:

First, I'd like to say that I am guilty of the crimes of first-degree murder, kidnapping, and robbery against Mr. and Mrs. Sumner. My reason for wanting to address the Court today is because of the many lies I told to everyone years ago at pretrial and then trial. I downplayed my involvement to look as if I were not guilty but the truth is that—the truth is that it was my idea to do this. Truly, I did not make anyone do anything. All were willing participants but I was, in fact, the leader. It was my idea to do it. I lied to this Court all throughout my trial testimony, same to [defense counsel and the State]. Even more so I lied to the people who deserve the truth the most, the family of Mr. and Mrs. Sumner, and for that, I am deeply sorry. There are no words that I could ever offer that would convey the depth of my remorse or sorrow, but again I say that I am truly sorry for what I have done and though I'm undeserving, I do ask forgiveness. My desire today is to reconcile the truth to the family of Mr. and Mrs. Sumner and to Your Honor, the attorneys and to the Court record. If necessary, I will answer any and all questions fully and truthfully. Thank you.

His conviction was upheld. Tiffany, Michael, Alan, and Bruce remain in jail today, with the former three on death row.

"It's sad," said Rhonda Alford about her parents. "It took them so long to find each other." Carol and Reggie's ashes sit in an urn in Rhonda's home, forever mixed and blended together.

DRUG CRAZED KILLER : THE TRUE STORY OF ROSIE ALFARO

ELIZABETH MARKS

Maria del Rosio Alfaro, better known to the media a Rosie Alfaro, is the first woman to be sentenced to death in Orange County. Her story is a tragic one, set in a town nearby Disneyland in Anaheim, California. By the time that Rosie was thirteen, she was heavily into drugs and considered by many to be an addict. At this age, Rosie was often doing fifty speedballs a day for weeks at a time, a speedball being a mixture of heroin and cocaine. Regular doses of this highly addictive cocktail were just the first steps along a dark path, and in grade seven she dropped out of school. By the time that Rosie was fourteen years old, she had become a prostitute. Despite efforts from her mother to get her back on track, a tormented and abused past pushed her forward on her path of self-destruction

At the witness stand in a court case only a few years after this point in her life, an old friend of Rosie's Tamara Benedict testified that at that time they both often slept with drug dealers for money so that they could buy drugs. Sometimes just receive their payment in narcotics directly. Benedict claimed "we had no jobs at all" and "sometimes we would steal from stores or get someone to steal for us." By the time that Rosie was fifteen, she was a single mother. At 18, she was a mother of two and pregnant with twins. It is also at this age that she committed the murder that would ruin her life.

When Rosie had been pregnant with her second child, she had spent some time living at the Wallace residence, the family of one of her friends from school. The Wallace's had three girls, Amber, April, and Autumn. Rosie was friends with April Wallace and was taking shelter at their house during one of the most difficult periods of her life. After her time living with the family, she got back into drugs, became distant, and had very little contact. The only time that she would have any association with the family would be when she was offered a lift somewhere.

A year later, when Rosie had had the baby and was pregnant with the twins, she was living with a relative of the father from her most recent pregnancy. This house was three blocks away from the Wallace residence. Rosie was on another drug binge at the time and had her first hit at eleven in the morning. By 2 PM she was getting desperate for another fix. She began to think about how she could acquire the money for more drugs. She mentioned to the men that she was with, the three of them looking after her oldest child, that she had an old video camera that she had left at the Wallace residence. She asked them to drive her to the residence so that she could retrieve it, and that she would gladly trade this camera in for cash so that they could all get another hit. The two men, Rosie, and her eldest boy who was only fourteen months old at the time drove to the Wallace residence. Rosie got out by herself to go and knock at the door, and the two men stood outside of the car with the baby. Rosie has made different testimonies in her time, both claiming that she didn't know that nine-year-old Autumn Wallace would be home and that she did realize. Whichever of these is true, Rosie knocked on the front door and Autumn answered. Based on her testimonies, it is more likely that she was expecting Autumn to be home so that somebody would enable her to get inside of the house.

Autumn's school had had an 'early day' that afternoon, and they had let the children leave at 2:35PM. Her mother wasn't due home from work until after five, and neither of her sisters were home. Rosie asked if she would be able to use their bathroom to fix her hair and freshen herself up. Autumn, who remembered Rosie from the time that she spent living with the family, didn't hesitate to let her in. Before Rosie had knocked at the door, Autumn had been cutting out paper dolls. She went back to her task in the living room. On her way to the bathroom, Rosie went to the kitchen and picked up a knife. In the bathroom, she created a ruse to trick Autumn. She claimed that she needed assistance with an eyelash curler, and asked Autumn to come into the bathroom to help her. When Autumn entered the bathroom, Rosie grabbed her. "That's when I did it," Alfaro told the investigators. "I stabbed her . . . 'cause she knew who I was," Rosie claims that Autumn made no sound when she was attacked and that nobody else was involved. "I was too high; I just remember her looking at me," Alfaro when she was interviewed at Orange County Jail. "Before, sometimes at night, the day would come back, and I'd block that out. Now I think about it more and more, because blocking is not working." Alfaro attacked Autumn with such ferocity that she died on the spot.

In all of Rosie's later testimonies, she claims that she was forced to stab the girl by one of the men who had accompanied her. She also claims that she stabbed Autumn several times, but that she did not finish the deed. Whether Rosie acted alone or with this man who she still refuses to identify, Autumn Wallace was stabbed fifty-seven times in her face, chest, and back. After this time, Rosie claims that she and the man went around the house stealing a few items. They took a portable TV, a typewriter, a telephone and a Nintendo set. Later on, they sold these items for a mere $300. As Rosie began to come down off her high, she realized the severity of the things that she had done and the guilt began to set in. She began to panic, and it was then that she made plans for her escape.

At 5:15 PM, April Wallace returned home. She found the door unlocked and the house in a mess. She called out to Autumn but got no response. She immediately ran to the house across the street for safety where she could wait for her mother to come home. Linda Wallace, the girls' mother, arrived home at 5:40 PM. She was told that her house had been burgled and that Autumn was missing. Believing that her girl might be hiding, she went inside the house to search for the youngest daughter and found her in the back bathroom in a pool of blood. Neighbors told Linda that they had seen a brownish Monte Carlo parked outside of the Wallace house and that two men were standing outside of the car. One of them was holding a small child. Police fingerprinted the house and found prints that matched Alfaro's. They brought Rosie in for questioning, and she denied any involvement in the murder, or that she has been near the house at all.

As they didn't have any further evidence or a witness that could identify her having been at the house, Rosie was let go.

At some point after the murder, Rosie asked one of her friends if she could leave a bag full of clothing outside of their house. She had made plans to leave for Mexico the next day, and wanted this bag to be easily accessible. However, Rosie never showed up. Investigators found out about the bag and inside they found a pair of Alfaro's tennis shoes and a pair of April Wallace's boots stolen from the house. They put out a warrant of arrest for Alfaro, and brought her in for questioning again. It was at this point that Alfaro began to realize that she wouldn't get away with the crime, and that she would have to be more cooperative with the police.

Alfaro identified one of the men that she had been with as Antonio Reynoso, being the man who stayed in the car with her son. Antonio had been released from prison the previous day. He had agreed to share his drugs with Rosie is she was happy to share her needle. The other man, who Rosie claims was active in the killing of Autumn Wallace, she has persistently refused to identify over the years, and only refers to by the name of Beto. Alfaro has said several times in court that she is not able to identify this man for the police as she fears for the safety of her children and her partner. Even if the face of the death penalty, Rosie did not reveal the identity of this man, and he still remains a mystery. Some members of the court have claimed that they feel the story of Beto is a fabrication, and that Rosie committed the crime by herself. However, there is some evidence to suggest that her claims might be true. Not only did neighbors see the two men out the front of the house, but a footprint in the bathroom that was initially thought to belong to Rosie was found to not match the shoes that she had been wearing. While all of the prints had initially been assumed to be Alfaro's, criminologist Marc Taylor found that there was also another set of prints both inside and outside of the house. This gives some credibility to Alfaro's story, but her unwillingness to identify the man means that she is taking the full consequences for the situation alone. Alfaro claims that when Beto saw that Autumn was home, he became enraged and put a knife to Rosie's back. He threatened to stab her if she wasn't going to stab Autumn. Rosie admits to stabbing Autumn several times, but maintains that Beto was the one who did the majority of the stabbing and caused Autumn's death. "If I wasn't so scared my family would get hurt, I'd tell the truth, but I just can't," she said in court. Even though it means that she is potentially getting the death sentence for a crime that she didn't solely commit, she remains silent on this issue in order to protect her family.

As Rosie plans to die with the identity of Beto, it is likely that this person will never be brought to justice and remains at large. Rosie initially claimed that the man was a friend of her father's, and that his name was Miguel. Later she claimed that this was not true and that the man who she would only name as Beto had a woman's name tattooed on the side of his neck. Alfaro identified a photo of the man. Orange County investigator Robert Harper identified the likely identity of this man to be Robert Frias Gonzalez, but Rosie gave no confirmation of this suspicion. It was later revealed the that tattoo on the side of his man's neck was actually a butterfly, but due to Rosie's state of mind and drug abuse her claims have not been judged as entirely false. It is impossible to say whether Rosie was identifying a photograph just to appease the police, and that this explains the difference between the tattoos, whether she was in such a state of mind that she couldn't remember the tattoo correctly, or whether the man had any identifiable tattoos done over with larger and darker designs to hide what was underneath. The fact that there is a discrepancy between the tattoos certainly doesn't factor this final consideration. Perhaps if his tattoo was the name is a lost loved one, he marked it with a butterfly to keep his display of respect? A deputy sheriff at the Orange County jail testified that he had seen a man similar to the one that Rosie had identified in the picture getting into a blue Camaro outside of the Orange County jail. From the evidence, it would certainly seem that another person was present at the residence and may have had involvement in the murder of Autumn Wallace, but without Alfaro's testimony on this matter nothing more can be pursued.

In the courtroom Alfaro, wearing a floral blouse and blue stretch pants, cried throughout Tamara Benedict's testimony and also those of her childhood friends, her boyfriend Manuel Cueva, and her mother Silvia Melendez Alfaro. When Cueva described the visits of Alfaro's children to the County jail as Rosie awaited trial, she openly sobbed. Sylvia Alfaro made every attempt possible to try to create some sympathy and understanding for Rosie, painting an image of the horrific childhood that she had suffered through. Sylvia testified that her husband was a dreadful alcoholic who regularly hit her and Rosie in front of the other children in the family. He would also often throw the whole family out of the house when he was in a drunken rage. Alfaro's mother discussed Rosie's early drug use and how she seemed totally unable to quit her habits, constantly seeking to get some distance from the real world. When Rosie was pregnant with her first child at the age of fourteen, her father left home and abandoned the family. Sylvia claimed that Rosie completely lost control of her drug addiction at the age of fifteen. "She wore heavy makeup, black clothes and was always dirty. She didn't care how she looked." From this point until when Rosie attacked Autumn, she was in an almost constant state of pregnancy. With no other way to support her habit, she slept with her dealers and attempted to look after her children as best she could.

A mental health expert, Dr. Consuelo Edwards, was the first one that Rosie had told about Beto. It was Edwards that recommended that she should speak about Beto in court, and he also came forward to defend her with his testimony. From his interactions with Rosie, Edwards deemed that her intellectual functioning was 'borderline' and that he feels that she has a serious learning disability. He didn't argue that he felt this excused any of her behavior, but that it should be something to factor when the jury are arriving at their decision. He tested Rosie as having an IQ of 78, and testified that her intellectual issues were made worse by the traumatic experiences that she had gone through as a child. In reaction to these claims, the prosecutor called forth several employees at the Orange County jail who testified to Rosie's poor behavior in jail. These employees also claimed that they had heard Rosie saying "I'm a frustrated person who takes things out on people, and have to learn to live with that," and "I'm not going to be able to do this again. I'm no actor. I'm going to be cold this time. I just want to get this over with." It is not certain whether this was a move to try to paint Rosie as an inherently bad or disturbed person, as this claims as nothing to do with her capacity intellectually. Perhaps they were making the argument that Rosie's lack of intellectual giftedness mean that she wasn't able to reflect on her own behavior and that way that she treated others. However these testimonies were intended, they painted Rosie as incredibly difficult to deal with and as somebody who lashes out with quick and ill-thought-through responses.

The first jury that assessed the case was on 14th July 1992. The judge for this case claimed that her crime was the most "senseless, brutal, vicious, and callous killing" that he had ever known. The jury was a deadlock with 10:2 in favor of Rosie receiving the death penalty, meaning that this was not enough to hand down the sentence. A deadlock means that the required amounts of votes was not reached, and in order to place a person on Death Row every member of the jury needed to agree that this was the proper course of action according to the evidence that they had viewed during the case. When Rosie was reflecting on this outcome and how close she had come to being sentenced to death, she claimed that "I do think that someone has to pay for what happened to that poor little girl, and that's me," she said. "But I can't help thinking how my life stopped, ended, at 18, and that I have no future, and all that is because of drugs." In many ways, Alfaro has distanced herself not only from the person that she was when she committed the crime, but the person who engaged in the type of lifestyle that she did before that. As she awaited her next trial date, she claimed that she would spend all day trying not to think about how likely it was that she would be sentenced to death and instead thought about the ways in which drugs had wasted her life.

Then in 2007, another court hearing was held where the jury placed forward the unanimous decision for the death sentence. During this trial, Rosie claimed that she was constantly haunted by her actions. She read out a letter that she had written to Autumn. "I have a picture of you in my Bible, and every time I open it, I see your innocent face and I think of my boys and what I would do if something were ever to happen to them. . . . So please know that I am deeply and truly sorry, Autumn, and I will pay for the rest of my life for what happened." Nobody can be sure whether this was an attempt to show remorse and soften the approach of the jury or whether Alfaro simply felt the need to be able to express these feelings in a more public context than she was capable of in jail. Perhaps Alfaro wanted for the Wallace family to hear that she was experiencing remorse over the issue, and that she was making a genuine attempt to comprehend and suffer for the things that she had done. When the sentence was handed down, Deputy Dist. Atty. Charles J. Middleton described the jury's decision as "justified" and claims that he knew the outcome based on the amount of time that the jury took considering the evidence, saying "I was sure it was a death verdict because I could not imagine 12 people agreeing that soon that this kind of a crime should not get a death sentence." These jury members deliberated for just over two days before they released their unanimous recommendation. When the sentence was handed down, it was met with clapping and cheering from the Wallace family and gasps and shock from the Alfaros and their supporters. Alfaro later claimed: "I know it's hard for the Wallaces to forgive me, and I don't ask for their forgiveness," Alfaro said. "If it had been one of my kids that was killed—I'm a mother too—I'd probably do the same thing: celebrate." William M. Monroe, who was Alfaro's attorney, quoted Alfaro as saying "I can't believe this. It can't happen to me. . . . Why did they (jurors) do this?" after the sentence was brought down. Monroe also made some emotional claims, seemingly unable to believe that Alfaro was truly going to be placed on Death Row. "I'm probably as shocked by the verdict as Rosie Alfaro is," Monroe said outside the courtroom. "I still contend that this crime was committed by a person with an abandoned and malignant heart, and Rosie Alfaro is not (such) a person." Monroe mentioned that "I feel terrible, absolutely terrible for what happened to Autumn Wallace, but this little girl, this young woman-child, does not deserve" and that he would file an appeal. After the verdict was served, photographers and cameramen were crowded around the courthouse hoping to catch a glimpse of the grief-ridden Alfaro. Alfaro supporters shielded their faces and turned their backs in an attempt to avoid the media. "Nobody wants to talk right now. We have no words," said a friend of the defendant. As with all cases, there was a lot of initial hype but it slowly died down. Now, when searching about the Alfaro case, there is rarely a recent article that will give any updates or further information on the matter. Rosie is simply on Death Row awaiting her visit to the gas chamber as her sons continue to grow up without her presence.

Much of the coverage around the case has regarded the behavior and quotes of the two mothers in the courtroom: Linda Wallace the mother of the deceased Autumn who claimed to fight for justice for her daughter's death, and Sylvia Alfaro who was fighting for the life of her own daughter. Linda Wallace made an emotional plea to the courtroom, claiming that during the trial her daughter has only been known as a young victim stabbed to death by somebody that she trusted. The grieving mother wanted everybody to know what Autumn was really like, and that was she so much more than the court case had reduced her to. She spoke about her blonde hair and brown eyes, and that she was an A student who loved swimming and fishing. She was incredibly creative, and wanted to be an artist when she grew up. Of Rosie, Linda claimed that what she did is horrible and that she will "never forgive or forget her." To Sylvia Alfaro, Linda said that she really felt for her because she knows what it feels like to lose a daughter.

Sylvia Alfaro was similarly trying to expand the way that the people in court were viewing her daughter, saying that "The first time that I came here, I felt like I was sitting in the electric chair," she cried. "I beg you, please forgive my daughter and please forgive what she did," Sylvia claimed that Rosie's issues with drugs had gotten a lot worse after the birth of her daughter's first son Daniel, and that she had enrolled her daughter in several drug programs in an attempt to beat her habits. Unfortunately, she always went back to her old ways after a few months. However, Sylvia maintains that while Rosie was pregnant she usually managed to control her drug addiction. This does not align with the information that was presented before the court on the day of Autumn Wallace's murder. This particular binge might well have been an isolated event or even an extended period of drug usage, but in either case, it would have been difficult for the jury to believe that Rosie was not a drug user during pregnancies when the entire case revolved around her desperation for another hit. Sylia had even gone so far as to sent her daughter to Mexico to live with her grandmother in the hope that this distance and change of environment would help her to get away from the complicated lifestyle around drugs, but this change in location didn't make any difference. She ended up coming back home when her grandmother was not able to cope with her behavior, and she fell into the same patterns.

Monroe, the attorney, attempted to raise some sympathy for Rosie regarding her troubled past and attempted to make the case that she should be sent to prison instead of the gas chamber. He made this assertion based on her addiction to drugs and her being the mother of four young boys. He claimed that the jury made a mistake in their recommendation, and he also introduced the notion of race. Monroe claimed that the mainly white jury could not possibly understand what it was to grow up in a household like Rosie had, and that they could not "empathize, understand or relate" to Latino women trapped in the drug world. While it might be true that somebody in a very different demographic cannot fully understand the life of somebody who has endured so much pain, the purpose of a jury is to find a random sampling of people who can determine what they feel is just action and what behavior should be acceptable in our society. Regardless of Alfaro's abuse in her childhood and early teens, the murder of a nine-year-old girl is not something that the jury considered as acceptable behavior.

Linda Wallace and her daughters had been traveling from their new homes in Lake Havasu , Arizona, the girls both having married and started their own families. April Nunez and Amber Szabo had been traveling in support of their deceased sister and trying to come to terms with her loss. In one interview, their mother Linda claimed that "You would think after all this time, you would get over it, but you don't." When asked how she endured through a trial, two penalty hearings, and a fifteen-year wait for the appellate review, Linda claimed that "I was doing it for Autumn." Later she also claimed that "it's the only thing I can do for her," the mom said, "I need to be there to represent her because she can't do it. I go to be with my daughter." Linda Wallace has also confided in several interviews how she feels outside of the court. "The hardest thing for me is to see people now who are Autumn's age," she said. "Not being able to see her grow up, that's what bothers me the most. She would be 26 years old now. She could be married. She could have kids. That's what I think about." Linda says that she has spent the years waiting for justice, and not spending her time or energy thinking about Alfaro. "I know she is in a bad place," Wallace says. "I know she will never see the light of day. I am fine with it." Linda also commented that Alfaro hasn't had much of a life since her arrest: "she just exists," the mother said. "It wouldn't be any life I would want." While the Wallace mother was one of the members of the family who was clapping when the sentence was passed down and has also been somebody to proclaim often and loudly that her daughter needs justice, she has also stated that she doesn't feel the need for Alfaro to be executed. In some ways, this might be an attempt to show a soft side to the media as in many of her interviews she claims that she waited fifteen years for the sentence to be handed down, when Alfaro had been imprisoned for that entire duration. This suggests that, in some way, Linda Wallace did feel that it was necessary for Rosie to be put on Death Row to properly avenge Autumn's death.

April and Amber have expressed similar long-lasting hatred of Rosie. "We get nothing," Zabo said. "And she gets all of these things. It makes me mad. ... I just want to see her be put to death, and I want to see it faster than it is taking." When April was asked if she would travel to San Quentin Prison to watch Alfaro get executed, she said "Oh yes, I would go to watch her die, without a doubt. I would do it myself if they'd let me." Linda Wallace was also asked in the same interview, she responded "I am not that much for that," she said. "If she is put to death, then another mother loses her child. I know what it feels like to lose a child." But her other interactions with the media suggest that Rosie getting the death penalty gave her some sense of relief and faith in the system.

The judge, Middleton, claimed that Monroe did not give any credence to Monroe's claims of racial misconception, and asserted that the jury had made their decision purely based on facts. He went on to say that she made her own choices in life and that Rosie cannot blame her action on others no matter how poor her treatment as a child and young adult had been. He also put forward the opinion that based on the evidence in court he did not believe that Rosie Alfaro was capable of looking after her children. Alfaro was convicted of first-degree murder with special circumstances, the circumstances being that the murder offered during the felonies of Burglary and Robbery. Alfaro joined two other women on Death Row, Maureen McDermott and Cynthia Lynn Coffman. McDermott was a Los Angeles registered nurse who was convicted in 1990 of hiring a co-worker to murder her roommate. It was found that Maureen planned to collect on a $100 00 mortgage insurance policy. Coffman was convicted in 1986 of the kidnapping and murder of a woman in San Bernardino. Capital punishment was restored in California in 1978, and these are the only three women to receive the death penalty in that time.

Since she was handed down the death sentence, Alfaro says that she spends her time thinking about how misguided her drug addled youth was, what happened to Autumn, and the days when her children will be old enough to know what she did. "God, I hate to think of the future, because there's not a future for me and my kids," she said. "It's going to be up to (them) if they still want to call me mom when they find out. I know they're going to find out sooner or later, and I'm scared of what they're going to decide." Alfaro is now 44 years old and still on Death Row with his four children still being cared for by boyfriend Cueva. She will not get to see them grow up, and may not feel that she deserves to give them any guidance in doing so. In many ways, she is now waiting for death as she no longer has a functional life. Waiting for the nightmare to be over do that she no longer has to block out the deeds of her past.

www.ingramcontent.com/pod-product-compliance
Lightning Source LLC
Chambersburg PA
CBHW021443150726
47989CB00001B/378